NEOLIBERALISM'S DEMONS

NEOLIBERALISM'S DEMONS

On the Political Theology of Late Capital

ADAM KOTSKO

Stanford University Press
Stanford, California

Stanford University Press
Stanford, California

Printed in the United States of America on acid-free, archival-quality paper

Library of Congress Cataloging-in-Publication Data

Names: Kotsko, Adam, author.
Title: Neoliberalism's demons : on the political theology of late capital / Adam Kotsko.
Description: Stanford, California : Stanford University Press, 2018. | Includes bibliographical
    references and index.
Identifiers: LCCN 2018003014 (print) | LCCN 2018007386 (ebook) | ISBN 9781503607132 |
    ISBN 9781503604810 (cloth : alk. paper) | ISBN 9781503607125 (pbk. : alk. paper)
Subjects: LCSH: Political theology. | Neoliberalism—Philosophy. | Economics—Philosophy.
Classification: LCC BT83.59 (ebook) | LCC BT83.59 .K68 2018 (print) | DDC 320.51/3—
    dc23
LC record available at https://lccn.loc.gov/2018003014

Cover design: Rob Ehle
Cover illustration: composite from iStock imagery by Rob Ehle

CONTENTS

ACKNOWLEDGMENTS

This study extends some of the arguments presented in my previous book, *The Prince of This World*, and to that extent could be understood as a sequel or follow-up. At the same time, it does not presuppose any knowledge of its predecessor—a fact that I verified empirically by presenting the basic argument put forward here in a series of lectures prior to the publication of that work. I would like to thank the following people for the generous speaking invitations that made it possible for me to develop these ideas: Joel Crombez (University of Tennessee at Knoxville), Monique Rooney (Australian National University), Julian Murphet (University of New South Wales), Robyn Horner and David Newheiser (Australian Catholic University), Bryan Cook and Catherine Ryan (Melbourne School of Continental Philosophy), Mike Grimshaw and Cindy Zeiher (Canterbury University), Campbell Jones (Auckland University), Harold Stone (Shimer College), Jared Rodríguez and Matthew Smith (Northwestern University), and Colby Dickinson (Loyola University Chicago). In addition to my hosts, many other interlocutors have pushed my thinking on this project. Among those not already named, I would like to highlight the contributions of Virgil Brower, Peter Hallward, Ted Jennings, Anna Kornbluh, James Martel, Knox Peden, and especially Marika Rose, who generously read and provided detailed comments on the entire manuscript. I am grateful, as well, to Emily-Jane Cohen of Stanford University Press for her support of this project. Finally, I must express my gratitude to Natalie Scoles, not only for her support and companionship, but for the prescient suggestion that I should teach my first elective course on the devil—setting in train the intellectual journey that has led to this book. In this, as in so many other cases, she knew me better than I knew myself.

NEOLIBERALISM'S DEMONS

INTRODUCTION

Every academic critique of neoliberalism is an unacknowledged memoir. We academics occupy a crucial node in the neoliberal system. Our institutions are foundational to neoliberalism's claim to be a meritocracy, insofar as we are tasked with discerning and certifying the merit that leads to the most powerful and desirable jobs. Yet at the same time, colleges and universities have suffered the fate of all public goods under the neoliberal order. We must therefore "do more with less," cutting costs while meeting ever-greater demands. The academic workforce faces increasing precarity and shrinking wages even as it is called on to teach and assess more students than ever before in human history—and to demonstrate that we are doing so better than ever, via newly devised regimes of outcome-based assessment. In short, we academics live out the contradictions of neoliberalism every day.

The present investigation is also autobiographical in a more specific sense. It represents an attempt to think the three great catastrophes that have shaped my political awareness—the Iraq War, the Global Financial Crisis, and the installation of Trump as US president—together, as part of a single overarching phenomenon. As I discuss in my first chapter, this has rarely been done: the Bush debacle is most often viewed as an isolated and unrepresentative episode within the broader historical arc of neoliberalism, while Trump and analogous right-wing reactions in other countries are widely presented as a resurgence of social and political elements that have unac-

countably persisted despite being foreign to neoliberal logic. For reasons that
will become clear as my argument unfolds, I view such interpretations as
inadequate and unsatisfying. Accordingly, I have sought to develop a more
holistic account of the neoliberal era that renders apparent right-wing devia-
tions legible as an integral feature rather than an inexplicable holdover from
a previous era.

Yet this study is not itself a mere reaction to recent political events. It
builds on concepts and themes from my previous book, *The Prince of This
World*.[1] There, I undertook a genealogy of the figure of the devil with an
eye toward uncovering his legacy in the modern world. I argued that the
devil has to be understood as at once a theological and a political figure, who
plays an ever-changing but consistently decisive role in the strategies that key
Christian theologians have deployed to legitimate the Christian social order
in their respective eras. By the late medieval period, the devil had become a
necessary scapegoat who allowed God to avoid direct responsibility for evil
while also giving God the opportunity to enhance his glory by overcoming
evil with good.

Crucial to this strategy was the notion that the devil freely chose to rebel
against God. This claim served as the foundation of a moral paradigm in
which freedom, far from being the basis of creaturely dignity or fellowship
with God, is thought exclusively as a mechanism for generating blameworthiness. I designated this form of moral entrapment as "demonization," in
recognition of the fact that it is the means by which God generates demons
within the theological system itself. And I argued that modernity inherited
this demonizing notion of freedom as blameworthiness and laid it at the
foundation of its own strategies of self-legitimation.

Given my focus on the origin and history of the figure of the devil in pre-
modern thought, my claims about modernity operated at a very high level of
generality. This book represents an effort to provide a more detailed warrant
for my account of the devil's legacy through a concentrated study of one particular paradigm of modern secular governance, namely neoliberalism, which
I put forward as the paradigm in which the strategy of moral entrapment
that I call demonization has been pushed to its uttermost limits. Neoliberalism makes demons of us all, confronting us with forced choices that serve
to redirect the blame for social problems onto the ostensible poor decision

making of individuals. This strategy attempts to delegitimate protest—and ultimately even political debate as such—in advance by claiming that the current state of things is what we have all collectively chosen.

At the time that I began developing the core argument of this book in the middle of 2016, the neoliberal consensus seemed nearly unassailable. In the United States the arch-neoliberal Hillary Clinton was in the process of consolidating her victory over the social democrat Bernie Sanders, and Donald Trump, though already coasting toward the Republican nomination, still seemed to be a bizarre sideshow rather than a serious political force. Like everyone else—apparently including even Trump himself—I was shocked at the election result. As I tried to come to terms with the increasingly surreal political events that began to unfold in the wake of that awful day, the concepts I had been developing for this project proved helpful. At the same time, the changed political circumstances shed fresh light on the neoliberal order. Given my poor track record as a prognosticator, I do not pretend to predict how the so-called Age of Trump will play out, or indeed whether Trump will even still be president by the time this book is published. Yet I maintain that the very fact such a thing was possible reveals something important about neoliberalism, something that will continue to be true even if things ultimately go "back to normal" (i.e., the neoliberal status quo ante is restored) in the coming years.

What Is Neoliberalism?

One of the consequences of the 2016 US election that most directly impacts my project is the emergence of the term neoliberalism as an object of mainstream political debate. Unfortunately, the discussion has resulted in more confusion around a term that was already much contested, as defenders of Clinton have tended to claim that neoliberalism is nothing more than a term of abuse and that what Sanders supporters tar as neoliberalism is simply identical to conventional liberalism. These new developments compound the difficulties stemming from the idiosyncratic US usage of *liberal* to mean "moderately left of center" and the similarities between neoliberalism and the "classical liberalism" advocated by libertarians.

Thus, while I flesh out my own demonic definition of neoliberalism in the chapters that follow, some initial clarification is in order. I will begin with the relationship between neoliberalism and "classical" or laissez-faire liberalism. The latter term refers to the economic order that prevailed during the "long nineteenth century," during which all the major European powers were committed to the free operation of a global capitalist market. In this paradigm economics and politics are two separate realms that operate best when the state resists the urge to meddle in the economy. As Karl Polanyi shows in *The Great Transformation*,[2] the establishment and maintenance of the classical liberal order required considerable state action, and the state was continually forced to ameliorate the destructive effects of unfettered market forces through a series of more or less ad hoc measures. Yet compared with the dominant model that emerged in the United States and Western Europe in the wake of the Second World War, the state's role in relation to the economy was much more circumscribed in classical liberalism.

The First World War and subsequent cataclysms discredited the classical liberal model, whose promise of endless peace and prosperity (at least within the European sphere) failed spectacularly. As Polanyi shows, this collapse led to various experiments with more state-driven economic models, including Soviet Communism, Fascism and National Socialism, and Roosevelt's New Deal. The model that ultimately took hold in the major Western countries after the Second World War has gone under a number of different names, including social democracy or the welfare state. Within the United States it was for a time known, confusingly enough, as neoliberalism, in recognition of the ways that the market forces familiar from classical liberalism were being intentionally harnessed and redirected toward socially beneficial ends. Ultimately, despite this clear opposition to classical liberalism, the term *liberalism* (sans *neo-*) came to prevail as a designation for the postwar American political settlement—a strange state of affairs that continues to generate considerable confusion. In recognition of this shift in linguistic usage, the faithful remnant in the United States who, inspired by the pulp novels of Ayn Rand, advocated a straightforward return to the prewar laissez-faire order came to call themselves libertarians.

For the purposes of the present study, I have chosen to designate the postwar order as "Fordism." There are many reasons for this choice. From an academic standpoint it is a nod to the Marxist analysts who have shaped my understanding of the dynamics of capitalism in the twentieth century, and in

contrast to a name like "postwar liberalism," it has the benefit of defamiliariz-
ing the postwar model and emphasizing our historical distance from it. On a
more personal level it reflects my upbringing in the suburbs of Flint, Michi-
gan, a city that has been utterly devastated by the transition to neoliberalism.
As I lived through the slow-motion disaster of the gradual withdrawal of the
auto industry, I often heard Henry Ford's dictum that a company could make
more money if the workers were paid enough to be customers as well, a principle that the major US automakers were inexplicably abandoning. Hence
I find it to be an elegant way of capturing the postwar model's promise of
creating broadly shared prosperity by retooling capitalism to produce a consumer society characterized by a growing middle class—and of emphasizing
the fact that that promise was ultimately broken.

By the mid-1970s, the postwar Fordist order had begun to break down to
varying degrees in the major Western countries. While many powerful groups
advocated a response to the crisis that would strengthen the welfare state, the
agenda that wound up carrying the day was neoliberalism, which was most
forcefully implemented in the United Kingdom by Margaret Thatcher and in
the United States by Ronald Reagan. And although this transformation was
begun by the conservative party, in both countries the left-of-center or (in
American usage) "liberal" party wound up embracing neoliberal tenets under
Tony Blair and Bill Clinton, ostensibly for the purpose of directing them
toward progressive ends. With the context of current debates within the US
Democratic Party, this means that Clinton acolytes are correct to claim that
"neoliberalism" just is liberalism but only to the extent that, in the contemporary United States, the term *liberalism* is little more than a word for whatever
the policy agenda of the Democratic Party happens to be at any given time.

Though politicians of all stripes at times used libertarian rhetoric to sell
their policies, the most clear-eyed advocates of neoliberalism realized that
there could be no simple question of a "return" to the laissez-faire model.
Rather than simply getting the state "out of the way," they both deployed and
transformed state power, including the institutions of the welfare state, to
reshape society in accordance with market models. In some cases this meant
creating markets where none had previously existed, as in the privatization
of education and other public services. In others it took the form of a more
general spread of a competitive market ethos into ever more areas of life—so

that we are encouraged to think of our reputation as a "brand," for instance, or our social contacts as fodder for "networking." Whereas classical liberalism insisted that capitalism had to be allowed free rein within its sphere, under neoliberalism capitalism no longer has a set sphere. We are always "on the clock," always accruing (or squandering) various forms of financial and social capital.

Why Political Theology?

Thus neoliberalism is more than simply a formula for economic policy. It aspires to be a complete way of life and a holistic worldview, in a way that previous models of capitalism did not. It is this combination of policy agenda and moral ethos that leads me to designate neoliberalism as a form of political theology. As with the term neoliberalism, my fully articulated view of the latter term will unfold over the course of the entire argument of this book, and so I will again limit myself to addressing some initial sources of confusion.

Here the term theology is likely to present the primary difficulty, as it seems to presuppose some reference to God. Familiarity with political theology as it has conventionally been practiced would reinforce that association. Schmitt's *Political Theology* and Kantorowicz's *The King's Two Bodies* both focused on the parallels between God and the earthly ruler,[3] and much subsequent work in the field has concentrated on the theological roots of political concepts of state sovereignty. Hence the reader may justly ask whether I am claiming that neoliberalism presupposes a concept of God.

The short answer is no. I am not arguing, for example, that neoliberalism "worships" the invisible hand, the market, money, wealthy entrepreneurs, or any other supposed "false idol," nor indeed that it is somehow secretly "religious" in the sense of being fanatical and unreasoning. Such claims presuppose a strong distinction between the religious and the secular, a distinction that proved foundational for the self-legitimation of the modern secular order but that has now devolved into a stale cliché. As I will discuss in the chapters that follow, one of the things that most appeals to me about political theology as a discipline is the way that it rejects the religious/secular binary.

That binary conditions the way people think about theology, leading them to view it as a discourse that, in contrast with rational modes of inquiry like philosophy and science, is concerned exclusively with God, is based on faith claims as opposed to verifiable facts, and is ultimately always dogmatic and close-minded. Yet attempts to establish a qualitative distinction between theology and philosophy or science on these grounds fail completely. If discourse about God is the defining feature, then Aristotle, Descartes, and Newton must be dismissed as mere theologians. If unverifiable premises mark the difference, then Euclidean geometry is the vilest form of fundamentalism.

Coming at the problem from the other direction, theology has always been about much more than God. Even the simplest theological systems have a lot to say about the world we live in, how it came to be the way it is, and how it should be. Those ideals are neither true nor false in an empirical sense, nor is it fair to say that believers accept them blindly. Every such theological ideal ultimately comes to depend on cultural inertia, but it could not take root and spread in the first place if it were not appealing and persuasive. It is this world-ordering ambition of theology, which relies on people's convictions about how the world is and ought to be, that for me represents a more fruitful distinction between theological discourse and philosophical or scientific discourses, at least as the latter tend to be practiced in the contemporary world.

It is in this sense that I consider neoliberal ideology a form of theology—it is a discourse that aims to reshape the world. But here another question arises: why not simply call it an ideology? Why court misleading preconceptions about theology when an alternative exists? I answer that the term *ideology* carries its own preconceptions with it, which I am even more concerned to avoid. The term necessarily evokes the Marxist theory of ideology, which in its most simplistic forms maintains that ideology is merely a secondary effect of the development of the economic mode of production. This reductionism carries with it the implication that ideology, as an illusion propagated by the bourgeoisie, can be replaced by the true view of things, namely Marxist science. While the Marxist tradition has consistently tried to break free of this one-sided reductionism—an attempt that has often involved an engagement with theology, most famously in Althusser's evocation of Pascal in "Ideology and Ideological State Apparatuses"[4]—it remains an inescapable center of gravity for the theory of ideology. Moreover, as I will show in subsequent chapters, this reductionism has made it very difficult for

Marxist critics to grasp the distinctiveness of neoliberalism. Hence I chose a different path.

I will begin to lay out my own account of political theology in the first chapter, but I hope it is already clear that I conceive of the discipline as more than simply the study of parallels between political and theological concepts. On the most fundamental level, I regard political theology as the study of systems of legitimacy, of the ways that political, social, economic, and religious orders maintain their explanatory power and justify the loyalty of their adherents. I maintain that we have misunderstood neoliberalism if we do not recognize that it, too, is a system concerned with its own self-legitimation. In this respect the account of neoliberalism that comes closest to my approach is Will Davies's *The Limits of Neoliberalism*, which he describes as "a piece of interpretive sociology." This means that his study "starts from the recognition that neoliberalism rests on claims to legitimacy, which it is possible to imagine as valid, even for critics of this system. . . . The book assumes that political-economic systems typically need to offer certain limited forms of hope, excitement, and fairness in order to survive, and cannot operate via domination and exploitation alone."[5] Davies's sociological approach takes him into territories I am not trained to explore, including the internal culture of regulatory agencies tasked with implementing neoliberal policies. In my view he provides an irrefutable demonstration of the fact that neoliberalism really is a consciously embraced ideology that has worked its way through concrete institutions of governance, while at the same time accounting for the developments and apparent contradictions in neoliberal thought and practice over the last several decades.

The obvious difference in scope and approach between our respective projects, despite our similar starting point, highlights another feature that is central to my vision of political theology: its genealogical character. Simply put, political theology always takes the long view—indeed, to such an extent that other academic disciplines could rightly portray it as speculative and even irresponsible. In the case of the current study, for instance, I must confess that I am unable to empirically document the connection that I am positing between late medieval theology and contemporary neoliberal practices. But neither could anyone else, and that is because the types of large-scale narratives that political theology constructs are neither true nor false on a strictly empirical basis. Political theology seeks not to document the past, but to make it available as a tool to think with. It does not aim merely to interpret the present moment, but to defamiliarize it by exposing its contingency. In other words, political-theological genealogies are creative attempts to reorder our relationship with the past and present in order to reveal fresh possibilities for the future.

The Plan of the Work

So far, I have offered only provisional sketches of neoliberalism and political theology and the relationship I see between them. They should not be regarded as firm definitions but as points of reference to help orient the investigation. In the chapters that follow, I will not merely be filling in more detail on neoliberalism and political theology; rather, I will gradually redefine each in terms of the challenge presented by the other.

For this pairing is anything but obvious. On the one hand, most accounts of neoliberalism leave little room for the conventional themes of political theology—above all of the notion of state sovereignty, which has supposedly been eclipsed in the neoliberal order.[6] On the other hand, Schmitt's initial formulation of political theology omits and even denigrates the economic concerns that are ostensibly the sole concern of neoliberalism. In order to bring together neoliberalism and political theology, my first step is to show that the conventional themes of political theology emerge persistently in the existing accounts of neoliberalism, but are always viewed as an extrinsic and even surprising element that theorists tend not to account for in any systematic way. Then, coming at the problem from the other direction, I attempt to show that Schmitt's presentation of political theology is artificially narrow and to provide grounds in his text for a broader vision of the field that could include a phenomenon like neoliberalism. Without leaving aside political theology's traditional focus on the homologies between theological and political systems, this more general political theology would ask more explicitly about the source of those homologies—namely, the ultimately unanswerable question that is expressed theologically as the problem of evil and politically as the problem of legitimacy.

Thus a political-theological approach to neoliberalism would not ask about the role of the state or sovereignty so much as the ways that the neoliberal order justifies and reproduces itself as a structure of meaning and legitimacy. I argue that the key concept in neoliberalism's attempt at self-legitimation is freedom, which neoliberalism defines in deeply individualistic terms that render market competition the highest actualization of human liberty. Accordingly, my second chapter is devoted to making the case for overcoming political theology's traditional hostility toward the economic realm. Drawing on the work of Wendy Brown, Giorgio Agamben, and Dotan Leshem, I trace this binary opposition back to the work of Hannah Arendt, who famously opposes the two realms and privileges the political over the economic. I then argue that "Arendt's axiom" is false: there is no pregiven distinction between the political and the economic, and in fact each political theological paradigm—very much including neoliberalism—reconfigures that binary for its own ends.

In the third chapter I provide an account of neoliberalism as a political theological paradigm that governs every sphere of social life—not just the state and the economy, but religion, family structure, sexual practice, gender relations, and racialization—by means of a logic of demonization. This provides the foundation for my analysis, in the fourth chapter, of the reactionary populist wave represented by the Brexit vote and the Trump presidency. There I argue that, far from a radical break with neoliberalism, the populist wave is a kind of "heretical" variant on the neoliberal paradigm, which accepts its core principles and pushes them to almost parodic extremes. I then conclude with some reflections on the new concept of political theology that has emerged from this investigation and on the prospects for building a more humane and viable alternative to the neoliberal order.

Broadly speaking, the first half of the book has a much more methodological focus than the second half. I have therefore provided more detail in my summaries of the arguments of the first two chapters, in recognition of the fact that some readers who are more interested in neoliberalism than in political theology may wish to skip ahead to the third chapter. Those readers will presumably be able to make some kind of sense of my interpretation of neoliberalism and the populist reaction, but that interpretation never could have taken the form that it has without the theoretical labor undertaken in the first two chapters. Hence I hope that those who skip ahead will return to the more methodological reflections, if only to clarify the relationship of my view of neoliberalism with other major accounts.

CHAPTER I

THE POLITICAL THEOLOGY
OF LATE CAPITAL

Neoliberalism loves to hide. On the increasingly frequent but still rare occasions when the term appears in the mainstream media, it is always in the context of an introductory treatment.[1] Strangely, one can never assume that the educated public is already acquainted with the force that has deeply shaped public policy and economic outcomes for a generation or more in the major Western countries and much of the developing world. For its advocates, as for those shaped by the "common sense" of mainstream political discussion, it is not a particular ideology nor even an ideology at all. It is simply the way things are, the set of "realistic" policies that "work." This very invisibility is a measure of its power, and the fact that the word can now be uttered in public is a sign that its planetary sway is growing less secure.

The term itself is slippery. It is first of all a periodizing concept that names the political-economic model that grew out of the crisis of the postwar settlement known as Fordism; hence it is in principle purely descriptive. At the same time it is a conceptual weapon for left-wing critics who take aim at all that is oppressive and alienating in our present world. So on the one hand, one might observe, seemingly neutrally, that whereas Fordism favored high taxation to limit inequality, energetic regulation of industry to make sure it serves social goals, strong labor unions that help workers claim their fair share, and careful control of international trade to protect domestic industry, neoliberalism has tended to pursue the reverse in all these areas: reducing taxes to increase the capital available for investment, deregulation to subject firms to market discipline rather than bureaucratic control, flexible labor markets that maximize efficiency and profitability, and free trade that breaks down arbitrary national boundaries to prosperity. Yet even though I have attempted to present it in positive terms that neoliberals themselves would accept, the very designation of the latter agenda as "neoliberal" implies a negative judgment of those developments.

This halo of negativity results partly from the fact that *neoliberal* is almost never used as a term of self-designation—though here, as with seemingly every generalization about neoliberalism, there are exceptions. Most notably, one of the movement's greatest theorists and propagandists, Milton Friedman, used the term in something like its contemporary sense in his 1951 essay "Neo-Liberalism and Its Prospects."[2] In this short text Friedman laments that in his time "legislation is still largely dominated by the trend of opinion toward collectivism" (3) and that even where the right manages an electoral victory, its leaders are still "infected by the intellectual air they breathe" (4). Yet the collectivist faith has encountered undeniable obstacles, and Friedman is confident that a new trend in public opinion is beginning to develop, one that makes room for a return to the tenets of classical nineteenth-century laissez-faire liberalism but without that movement's naive antistatism. What Friedman describes in this lecture is identifiable as the contemporary neoliberal agenda, in which the state actively cultivates and maintains the conditions necessary for vigorous market competition, trusting in the price mechanism to deliver more efficient outcomes than direct state planning ever could. Hence his use of the term *neo*-liberalism: it is not a question of simply "returning" to traditional laissez-faire by getting the state out of the way, but of using state policy as a means to actively create a *new* version of classical liberalism.

Much in Friedman's text appears prophetic in retrospect, but one detail in particular is simply uncanny. In an offhand remark, he notes that "some twenty years or more may elapse between a change in the underlying current of opinion and the resultant alteration in public policy" (3). Right on schedule, one of the signal events in the transition from Fordism to neoliberalism happened twenty years after Friedman wrote his article: Nixon's decision in 1971 to go off the gold standard, which broke with the Bretton Woods settlement that had governed international finance throughout the postwar era and inadvertently cleared the space for the fluctuating exchange rates that proved so central to the rise of contemporary finance capitalism. Only two years later, the oil crisis ushered in the period of "stagflation," a combination of slow economic growth and high inflation that should not have been possible in terms of the regnant Keynesian economics of the time and that proved unresponsive to the standard mix of policies Keynesianism prescribed.

The moment for a new economic model had arrived, and the theorists and propagandists of neoliberalism—the group that Philip Mirowski calls the Neoliberal Thought Collective—were ready to seize the opportunity.[3] And once they gained ascendancy, they set up a self-reinforcing system that not only persisted but expanded for decades. Even the Global Financial Crisis, far from toppling the neoliberal order, strengthened its stranglehold on the terms of debate, despite the fact that no major economist had predicted it and most neoliberal policy prescriptions actually worsened the economic slump they were meant to solve. Admittedly, this amazing prescience and persistence is difficult to square with the tenets of neoliberal theory, which in popular presentations appears to amount to a simplistic libertarianism that would seem more at home in a college dorm room than in the most prestigious economics departments in the world. But in another turn of the screw, the neoliberal order has given rise to financial engineering of mind-boggling complexity, deploying the expertise of PhD physicists and massive computing power to gain a competitive edge in the market.

Thus neoliberalism is both a descriptive and a polemical term to describe an ideology whose adherents mostly refuse to admit that it exists, which is at once stunningly foresighted and vulnerable to unpredictable crises and which was masterfully implemented by Machiavellian geniuses who often appear to be as intellectually sophisticated as a teenager who has just discovered Ayn Rand. Clearly, we are dealing with a strange phenomenon, and the academic literature surrounding neoliberalism reflects the contradictions in its elusive object. While the basic content of neoliberalism—both its ideological agenda and the results that follow from it—is not subject to serious dispute, no settled agreement exists on how to articulate those features into a coherent whole. To illustrate my point, I will briefly present a few of the most influential approaches to this question.

David Harvey's strategy, in *A Brief History of Neoliberalism*, is to put forward the concrete results as the key to interpreting neoliberalism.[4] From Harvey's Marxist perspective, neoliberalism is the latest front in the class struggle, undoing the postwar gains of the working class through the formation and enrichment of a new capitalist class and the immiseration of workers. Although Harvey does draw attention to the fact that neoliberalism has "become hegemonic as a mode of discourse" and has been thoroughly "incorporated into the common-sense way many of us interpret, live in, and understand the world,"[5] he ultimately dismisses the policy agenda as incoherent and the ideology as essentially irrelevant. Indeed, it is only the class element that is definitive of neoliberalism for Harvey, so that China—which is far from embracing the Washington Consensus on an ideological or policy level, as shown by the fact that it still promulgates communist-style five-year plans that imply a level of direct state planning completely incompatible with neoliberalism—can appear as an exemplar of neoliberalism due solely to the emergence of a new capitalist class in recent decades.[6] Yet if neoliberalism is simply the bourgeoisie's revenge, then how can Harvey account for the fact that it is precisely a new capitalist class that is created?[7] And how can he find a place for neoliberal thinkers like Friedman, those strange "organic intellectuals" who preexisted, and contributed to the creation of, the very class that their ideas came to serve?

It is this group that Mirowski highlights with his notion of the Neoliberal Thought Collective. One could walk away from Harvey's account viewing the major figures of neoliberalism as dispensable figureheads for impersonal political and economic forces. By contrast, the most compact possible summary of Mirowski's book would be: "It's people! Neoliberalism is made out of people!" In this reading there was nothing inevitable about neoliberalism's rise, which depended on the vision and organization of particular nameable individuals. For Mirowski, the apparent incoherence in neoliberal ideology and policy making is the product of the political strategy of the Neoliberal Thought Collective, which feeds the general public a simplified version of neoliberal dogma, providing its agenda with a veneer of popular legitimacy, while a more flexible and realistic esoteric doctrine guides the actual policy implementation. In other words, the discursive elements that Harvey tends to dismiss are an integral part of neoliberalism's initial political success and its ongoing self-reproduction.

For Wendy Brown, by contrast, the results that Harvey and Mirowski attribute to a political struggle are precisely the death of politics.[8] Inspired by Hannah Arendt's articulation of Aristotle's distinction between the political and the economic realms, Brown portrays neoliberalism as an attempt to extinguish the political—here represented by the liberal democratic tradition of popular sovereignty and self-rule—and consign humanity to a purely economic existence. In the end Brown calls us to take up a strange kind of metapolitical struggle against the economic enemy, in defense of politics as such. Meanwhile, Jodi Dean, who agrees that neoliberalism has a depoliticizing tendency, argues that this depoliticization actually depends on the notion of democracy and that appeals to democracy against neoliberalism are therefore doomed in advance.[9]

As ever, the Protean slipperiness of neoliberalism seems to defy analysis. Is neoliberal ideology a smokescreen for a political agenda, or is it integral to the whole? Is neoliberalism actually properly political at all, or does it instead spell the death of politics? Does neoliberalism undermine democracy, or does it rely on it for its own legitimation? What exactly are we dealing with here?

This situation is very strange. As I have already noted, for academic commentators, in stark contrast to the sometimes willful ignorance found in mainstream debate, the attributes and effects of neoliberalism appear more or less self-evident; that is to say, there should seemingly be no dispute about what neoliberalism is. Yet in what almost amounts to a parody of the atomistic individualism of our contemporary order, there sometimes seem to be as many concepts of neoliberalism as there are commentators. There is, however, a broad consensus on which theoretical tools are most helpful in this regard, insofar as the dominant perspectives for dealing with neoliberalism are Marxism (an obvious fit for a critique of contemporary capitalism) and Foucauldianism (equally obvious in light of Foucault's shockingly prescient account of the formative stages of neoliberalism in *The Birth of Biopolitics*).[10] Other approaches, such as psychoanalysis,[11] have made themselves felt in this debate, but Marxism and Foucauldianism remain the key points of reference in essentially every major treatment of neoliberalism.[12]

The present study is on one level no exception to this trend, insofar as I draw extensively on works from both traditions. Yet I will largely sidestep the Marx-Foucault debate by using a different interpretive framework as my starting point: namely, political theology. This move is admittedly counterintuitive on two levels. First, the meaning of political theology is arguably as contested as that of neoliberalism, if not more so; thus, I risk attempting to use the unknown to clarify the unknown. Second, within the literature itself, engagement with neoliberalism has often been taken to entail a rejection or subordination of the concerns most often associated with political theology.[13]

In what follows, I will not be arbitrarily asserting my own vision of political theology and then applying it to neoliberalism, nor will I be castigating previous analysts of neoliberalism for the supposed mistake of neglecting political theology. In point of fact, the meaning of political theology is unclear. This is not because people are unaccountably failing to grasp it but because from its very inception, the concept of political theology is entangled with a political agenda that is presented in an indirect and partially concealed manner—neoliberalism is not the only thing that loves to hide. This intentionally misleading rhetorical strategy has led to durable blind spots and deadlocks within the field of political theology itself, which have in turn created a situation in which diagnosticians of neoliberalism understandably do not see political theology as a suitable tool for their endeavors.

My goal in staging this largely missed encounter, then, is not only to demonstrate what political theology has to offer to the study of neoliberalism. I am equally concerned to develop a new and more capacious concept of political theology. My wager is that the encounter between political theology and neoliberalism—precisely because it is counterintuitive and seemingly unnatural—will provide a uniquely productive path toward a renewed political theology. To put it differently, if I want to use political theology as a tool to get at neoliberalism, I will need to rebuild and rearticulate the concept of political theology as I go. It is less a question of applying a method to an object than of taking up a particular object in order to force changes in the method.

This chapter will lay the groundwork for this mutual illumination of political theology and neoliberalism. After giving an overview of political theology as it is generally understood in contemporary academic debates, I will provide a basic account of how this relatively narrow vision of political theology (and the themes taken to be most directly related to it) have fared in discussions of neoliberalism. I will then give a counterreading of Schmitt's foundational work *Political Theology*, demonstrating that the very text that gives rise to that constricted view also plants the seeds for a more flexible approach to political theology. Finally, I will sketch out an initial reading of neoliberalism not only as a possible object for political theology, but as an exemplary one.

Staging a Missed Encounter

Hearing the term political theology for the first time, one would likely be drawn to two possible hypotheses about its meaning. On the one hand, one might assume that political theology means politically engaged theology. Depending on one's perspective, sympathetic examples may spring to mind, such as the theology of Martin Luther King Jr., or Latin American liberation theology, or perhaps more reactionary options like the theology of the US religious right. In either case it would be a question of carrying theologically based normative claims into the political realm. On the other hand, political theology may evoke phenomena of quasi-religious fervor directed at political figures and movements, such as a "personality cult" around a charismatic leader. Thus, political theology could refer either to religiously informed political action or to practices that seem to treat politics as a religion.

Both of these definitions are attested in the literature. For instance, Jacob Taubes's lecture course *The Political Theology of Paul* presents the Apostle as a theologically motivated rebel against Roman hegemony. Taubes claims that "the Epistle to the Romans is a political theology, a *political* declaration of war on the Caesar," and that "Christian literature is a literature of protest against the flourishing cult of the emperor."[14] The latter cult would in turn represent a political theology of the inverse variety.

With these two possible meanings in mind, we could say that political theology, as an academic discipline, is concerned with all crossings between the political and the theological realms, in either direction. The guiding assumption of political theology as a research program is that such crossings are not rare or remarkable, but in fact happen all the time—including in the ostensibly secular modern world. The central methodological credo is encapsulated in this frequently quoted passage from Schmitt's *Political Theology*: "All significant concepts of the modern theory of the state are secularized theological concepts, not only because of their historical development—in which they were transferred from theology to the theory of the state, whereby, for example, the omnipotent God became the omnipotent lawgiver—but also because of their systematic structure, the recognition of which is necessary for a sociological consideration of these concepts."[15]

Though more recent studies have broadened their purview, most investigations in the realm of political theology have centered on the key examples given here by Schmitt: the parallel between God and the earthly ruler and the Christian lineage of modern political institutions. Both are at work, for instance, in Kantorowicz's classic *The King's Two Bodies*. Most of Kantorowicz's study is taken up with the ways in which medieval political theorists borrowed concepts from Christology to begin thinking of monarchy as an institution that exceeds the individual who happens to be king at any given time. Just as Christ has a divine nature that exists apart from the particular human form he took up in the Incarnation, the medieval theorists reasoned, so too does the king have a royal body that survives the death of his mortal human body. But the ultimate goal of the argument is to point out how these hybrid political-theological concepts unexpectedly informed the concept of "fictitious personhood," which is central to modern legal theory and practice.

In the context of modern secularism, premised as it is on the separation of the political and religious realms, the claims of political theology can appear scandalous. Though Schmitt and Kantorowicz were both decidedly right-wing thinkers, this element of scandal has proven durably appealing to those on the left—particularly Marxists, for whom the critique of religion is the beginning of all critique. Walter Benjamin was a pioneer here, citing Schmitt's *Political Theology* early on and going on to plan a (sadly unrealized) research project called "Capitalism as Religion."[16] By contrast, when liberal commentators attend to the claims of political theology, they tend to view the persistence of theological elements in modernity as a problem to be diagnosed and solved. The later work of Jacques Derrida, which aimed to defend the "perfectible" heritage of the Enlightenment, is a case in point. In response to John Caputo's *Prayers and Tears of Jacques Derrida*, which depicted Derrida as a quasi Christian, scholars such as Michael Naas and Martin Hägglund have argued that Derrida's investigations of theology always aim at continuing the work of secularization.[17] In this Derrida is typical of the so-called religious turn in continental philosophy, which represented an attempt to articulate a distinctive yet inclusive cultural heritage for the European Union.

Political theology rarely seemed more relevant than in the early 2000s, when the Bush administration claimed sovereign emergency powers that seemed to come straight out of Schmitt. *Political Theology* begins with the lapidary claim, "Sovereign is he who decides on the exception,"[18] which George W. Bush (presumably unwittingly) paraphrased in his inimitable style when he proclaimed, "I'm the decider." The state of exception inaugurated by 9/11 served as justification for a range of increasingly destructive decisions—to declare people enemies without due process, to torture and kill with impunity, to start an unrelated war in Iraq, even to reshape the fates of entire countries and regions. When combined with the officially denied and yet unmistakable atmosphere of a religious war between Islam and the Christian West, the conventional program of political theology appeared to be exactly the right theoretical tool for that historical moment. This was above all the case for the work of Giorgio Agamben, whose theory of the constitutive relationship between sovereign power and the production of readily victimizable "bare life" seemed prophetic of the worst excesses of Guantánamo Bay and Abu Ghraib.[19]

Early in Bush's second term, however, the aura of invincibility had begun to fade. Even as Bush proved unable or unwilling to cope with the domestic emergency of Hurricane Katrina, the Iraq War descended into the familiar quagmire from which the United States still has yet to disentangle itself. No longer could Bush claim to be the sovereign "decider" reshaping the world according to his will, and hence the tools of political theology came to seem, at the very least, less central to grasping our contemporary predicament. Neoliberalism gradually came to take the place of the sovereign exception in the politically engaged humanities, most urgently in the wake of the Global Financial Crisis.

Different thinkers characterized this shift in attention in different ways. Most strident and radical were Hardt and Negri, who took the failure of the Bush project as a vindication of their theory of the emerging global order they called Empire. In *Commonwealth*, the concluding volume of their influential trilogy, they devote a substantial section to a "Brief History of a Failed Coup d'État."[20] From their perspective, the Bush Doctrine represented not a permanent shift in global relations but an illegitimate attempt to seize power from the emergent configuration of Empire. While acknowledging Bush's destructiveness, they nonetheless chide those who bought into the neoconservative fantasy that the United States could impose its will on the world through military force. This attempted "coup" against the global order could not but fail, and in short order it did: "It took only a few years . . . for these ghostly figures to collapse in a lifeless heap. The financial and economic crisis of the early twenty-first century delivered the final blow to U.S. imperialist glory. By the end of the decade there was general recognition of the military, political, and economic failures of unilateralism."[21] This discussion of the Bush Doctrine could be taken as a culmination of the critique of political theology with which *Commonwealth* begins. Targeting Agamben specifically, Hardt and Negri suggest that exponents of political theology essentially buy into the state's own fantasy of itself, causing them to ignore the true operations of power. When political theory operates at this level, "what is eclipsed or mortified . . . is the daily functioning of constitutional, legal processes and the constant pressure of profit and prosperity. In effect, the bright flashes of extreme events and cases blind many to the quotidian and enduring structures of power."[22] In short, they claim, "We need to stop confusing politics with theology."[23]

In this context, Agamben's next major work was an ambiguous intervention. Originally published in 2007, *The Kingdom and the Glory* represented a decisive turn toward economic concerns.[24] If Hardt and Negri were to accuse him of "confusing politics with theology," this massive tome could be read as a preemptive rejoinder to the effect that we not only need to confuse politics with theology, but we need to confuse economics with theology as well. Although he never explicitly mentions neoliberalism in this text (or in any other published work to my knowledge), Agamben is clearly concerned to document the lineage of the indirect governance via economic means that is characteristic of our neoliberal era.[25] What is less clear is the relationship between the political theology he had advanced in earlier works and the economic theology he is laying out here. Indeed, he simply juxtaposes them as two distinct paradigms of governance without elaborating their relationship (is one a subset of the other? do they share a common root?), and in a move that I will discuss at length in the next chapter, he ultimately turns away from economic theology altogether in favor of an investigation of the role of "glory" in political theology.

Other commentators show a similar ambivalence. Though David Harvey does not refer explicitly to political theology, his treatment of the themes conventionally associated with it—both the state in general and the Bush-style neoconservative vision of the state in particular—is illustrative. On the one hand, he views the role of the state under neoliberalism as fundamentally incoherent and unsustainable, insofar as it must both guarantee the existence of markets and avoid illegitimately intervening in them. In some cases the way he characterizes this dilemma seems to echo a one-sided libertarianism more than a distinctively neoliberal position, above all in occasional pass-ing remarks where he treats financial bailouts as an obvious contradiction to neoliberal theory.[26] Under a hypothetically pure laissez-faire regime, bailouts would indeed be off-limits, but as Friedman had pointed out already in 1951, a simple return to that model is neither possible nor desirable. In reality, a generalized bailout of all major players—one that neither picks winners nor asserts direct government control over any of the individual firms—is the only possible response to a failure in the all-important financial sector, which serves as the market of markets under neoliberalism. Far from a contradic-tion, a financial sector bailout is precisely the duty of the neoliberal state as ultimate guarantor of market structures, which helps to explain the fact that every neoliberal regime has resorted to such tactics in the face of finan-cial crises. (And in a nice neoliberal twist, the US Treasury actually turned a modest profit on its bailout funds.)

On the other hand, Harvey presents neoconservatism—by which he means any kind of assertive nationalism, not only Bush's variation on the theme—as a kind of necessary supplement to neoliberalism. While neoliber-alism requires a strong state, its thoroughgoing individualism undercuts any traditional rationale for why the state deserves our loyalty and obedience. Nationalism, though distasteful from the cosmopolitan neoliberal perspec-tive, stands in the gap by providing a point of identification for citizens that would otherwise be lacking, and therefore Harvey can claim that "the neo-liberal state needs nationalism of a certain sort to survive."[27] Here we gain greater clarity about how the two logics (here termed neoconservatism and neoliberalism rather than political theology and economic theology) are related in practice, but on the conceptual level they are still juxtaposed as two distinct entities.

Coming at the relationship between the two paradigms from a different angle, several commentators have followed Agamben in linking neoliberalism to theology in general. Both Joshua Ramey and Joseph Vogl, for example, characterize neoliberal theory as a kind of contemporary theodicy, justifying the ways of the economy to man.[28] This connection has firm historical grounding: Agamben provides some evidence for an explicit genealogical link between traditional concepts of theodicy or divine providence and modern economics in the appendix to *The Kingdom and the Glory*, and Mark C. Taylor had already elaborated a much more detailed and rigorous genealogy in his 2004 work *Confidence Games*.[29]

By contrast, some connections between neoliberalism and theology are more metaphorical or impressionistic, as when Wendy Brown claims that neoliberalism demands "sacrifice": "As we are enjoined to sacrifice to the economy as the supreme power and to sacrifice for 'recovery' or balanced budgets, neoliberal austerity politics draws on both the religious and secular, political meanings of the term."[30] Yet if this is a theology, for Brown it cannot be a *political* theology, because even here the economic (austerity measures) has fully displaced the political (warfare): "as economic metrics have saturated the state and the national purpose, the neoliberal citizen need not stoically risk death on the battlefield, only bear up uncomplainingly in the face of unemployment, underemployment, or employment unto death."[31] Nonetheless, this theological element, just like the neoconservative reaction in Harvey's account, cannot be regarded as an intrinsic part of neoliberalism. Rather, it is "a supplement, something outside of its terms, yet essential to its operation."[32]

Again and again, the themes that clearly fall within the ambit of political theology—the state, its sovereign authority, the quasi-religious fervor excited by nationalistic identification, the demand for sacrifice—keep appearing, but always as a subordinate element, an unaccountable yet somehow necessary holdover, even as a surprise. It is somehow shocking, for example, that the neoliberal state continues to exercise emergency powers in an era when the

state is supposedly receding, and the endurance of neoconservative nationalism is also a puzzle that must be explained (or explained away as a purely
contingent fit of reactionary willfulness, as in Hardt and Negri).[33]

Yet the intimate connection between the two realms is hiding in plain
sight, namely, in the Bush administration's attempt to impose neoliberalism
on Iraq. This episode opens Harvey's study, and Brown devotes a lengthy
section to it, memorably entitled "Best Practices in Twenty-First-Century
Iraqi Agriculture." Here the retrograde avatars of neoconservatism, the
hapless advocates of the outmoded vision of state sovereignty, are rushing
to implement an extreme vision of the very neoliberalism that is supposedly superseding them. Once we see this connection, countless other details
of the Bush administration fall into place: its reliance on private military
subcontractors (making the Iraq War arguably the first fully neoliberal war
in human history), its market-based Medicare prescription-drug benefit,
its thwarted attempt to privatize Social Security. In many respects, then,
the Bush era continued the durable alliance between neoliberals and neoconservatives that had been so crucial to the rise of the neoliberal order
under Reagan,[34] while his use of sovereign emergency powers to export
neoliberalism abroad echoes previous events like Augusto Pinochet's 1973
coup, which led to a campaign of torture and "disappearances" in the service of brutally imposing a neoliberal program on Chile. More generally,
every neoliberal regime has witnessed the expansion of police powers and
surveillance—and in the United States in particular, this has led to a vast
intensification of the carceral state, implemented in part through innova-
tions in the private prison industry. Far from being simply juxtaposed, the
supposedly separate paradigms—whether we prefer to call them political
theology and theological economy or neoconservatism and neoliberalism—
are deeply intertwined, in a way that cannot be explained in terms of
anachronistic holdovers or extrinsic supplements.

Mapping the Blind Spots

The fact that Harvey and Brown both call attention to the Iraq example
without drawing the full consequences is more than a coincidence. If we take
them as exemplary of Marxist and Foucauldian approaches to neoliberalism,
respectively, this correspondence could serve to demonstrate that the same

features that render Marxism and Foucauldianism such obviously appropriate tools for analyzing neoliberalism also produce durable blind spots.

Broadly speaking, both theories, like their neoliberal object, deemphasize the autonomy and agency of the state. In traditional Marxism the state is not an autonomous power but merely a mechanism for intermediating the class struggle, hence part of the epiphenomenal "superstructure." Foucauldianism is much more concerned to integrate "knowledges" with the concrete practices of power, yet the signature gesture of Foucault's theory of power is "beheading the king," which is to say, displacing the pretensions of the sovereign state in favor of the fine-grained mechanisms of biopower. Hence Brown is able to do more than Harvey with the way neoliberal theory shapes the practice of everyday life, but neither provides an account of the state as integral to the neoliberal order. This is not to say that Marxists have not developed more robust accounts of the role of ideology and the state nor that Foucauldians have not challenged the apparently stark divide between sovereignty and biopolitics. When they take up neoliberalism, however, there seems to be little reason to resist the inertia of the antistatist tendencies in their respective theories. Theory and object seem like a perfect fit.

The blind spots of conventional political theology are, if anything, exactly the inverse. Although political theology shares Foucault's attention to theory or ideology, it strongly emphasizes the necessity and autonomy of the state. More than that, beginning with Schmitt, it has tended to assert the importance of the state over against the economic realm in specific. Even where his critics have rejected the outsized role Schmitt grants to the political, the qualitative distinction between the political and the economic has remained seemingly axiomatic. Thus, while political theology overcomes one of the founding binaries of secular modernity—that between the political and the religious—it relies heavily on the equally central binary of the political and the economic. Indeed, within the field of political theology, the dichotomy between the two realms is arguably more stark than in either Marxism or Foucauldianism.

Taking neoliberalism as an object for political theology will require us to break down that axiomatic binary, which is the task of the following chapter. Here I am concerned with a necessary preliminary step: to demonstrate that such a break with convention can nonetheless be seen as a development within the project of political theology. In fact, I believe that the same Schmitt who bequeathed the sharp political/economic dichotomy to political theology also provides us with resources for undermining it.

Above, I distinguish three senses of political theology: theologically informed political action, treating politics in quasi-religious ways, and the general study of such transfers between the political and theological realms. Schmitt's *Political Theology* is in some sense all three at once, particularly when read in conjunction with *The Concept of the Political*. There he defines the political as the realm where decisions are made about who is a friend and who is an enemy, and the state as whatever entity has the recognized authority to make such a decision. While the distinction of friend and enemy is certainly related to other binaries such as good and evil or beautiful and ugly, what distinguishes the political from other realms of life is that it "denotes the utmost degree of intensity of a union or separation, of an association or dissociation."[35] The most extreme expression of this intensity of the political is the declaration of war "in order to preserve one's form of existence."[36]

In other words, the political deals with things worth killing and dying for. This alone indicates that the political is the most important realm of human existence. It is also the most universal, because no merely particular pursuit can justify war—least of all economic motivations: "To demand seriously of human beings that they kill others or be prepared to die themselves so that trade and industry may flourish for the survivors or that the purchasing power of grandchildren may grow is sinister and crazy."[37] As the most serious and irreversible action that can be taken, war must stem from "an existential threat to one's way of life" as a whole.[38] Yet there is a sense in which the political is deeply particularistic, insofar as no one but the group in question can decide on the existence of such a threat, and no principle from outside the sphere of the political can justify its decision to go to war: "For as long as a people exists in the political sphere, this people must, even if only in the most extreme case—and whether this point has been reached has to be decided by it—determine by itself the distinction of friend and enemy. . . . The justification of war does not reside in its being fought for ideals or norms of justice, but in its being fought against a real enemy."[39] And in the last analysis, the political authority—commonly called the state, though other entities that we might recognize as religious or class-based could serve in this capacity—is that person or entity that has the recognized authority to make that determination and demand of members of the community that they kill and die.

It is in this context that we must understand the famous first line of *Political Theology*: "Sovereign is he who decides on the exception."[40] That is to say, whoever can decide whether a situation demands that the usual legal norms be put aside and exceptional action be taken is the sovereign authority in a particular political community. An exceptional circumstance could include a natural disaster or even an economic crisis, but it is clear that the exemplary sovereign decision is the decision to go to war—and so the sovereign is by definition the head of state. The sovereign need not make declarations of war or emergency in order to remain sovereign, but Schmitt emphasizes those exceptional situations because of his conviction that the exception is particularly revelatory. In *Concept of the Political*, for instance, while speaking of the fact that the existence of a political situation does not necessarily entail war, which is an exceptional last resort, Schmitt claims, "That the extreme case appears to be an exception does not negate its decisive character but confirms it all the more. . . . One can say that the exceptional case has an especially decisive meaning which exposes the core of the matter."[41] In other words, the very fact that political conflict could result in war shows how very serious a matter it is. This may seem a more or less commonsensical observation, but by the end of the first chapter of *Political Theology*, the exception takes on what we might call a more metaphysical flavor:

> Precisely a philosophy of concrete life must not withdraw from the exception and the extreme case, but must be interested in it to the highest degree. The exception can be more important to it than the rule, not because of a romantic irony for the paradox, but because the seriousness of an insight goes deeper than the clear generalizations inferred from what ordinarily repeats itself. The exception is more interesting than the rule. The rule proves nothing; the exception proves everything: It confirms not only the rule but also its existence, which derives only from the exception. In the exception the power of real life breaks through the crust of a mechanism that has become torpid by repetition.[42]

Here the usual relationship between exception and norm is reversed, but more than that, the exception is described in quasi-divine terms. The exception is more important than the rule; it founds and at the same time transcends the rule; and most strikingly, it grants life to a rule that would otherwise be dead and machinelike. It seems only a small step to use explicit theological language: the exception is the most high, the creator, the sustainer, the redeemer. This quasi-divine reality is for Schmitt the heart of the political realm.

Here we are clearly dealing with one particular sense of political theology: the theologization of the political. There is also a clear element of the converse sense of political theology, namely, the importation of theological norms into the political realm, insofar as Schmitt's political quasi divinity bears striking similarities to the traditional Christian God. For example, the political in Schmitt's sense is, like God, something that must necessarily exist. Though he periodically entertains thought experiments about the possibility of eliminating the political aspect of human life, he concludes by flatly declaring: "State and politics cannot be exterminated."[43] And throughout the text he argues that the liberal attempt to do away with the political and abolish war will necessarily backfire in the form of ever more destructive wars.

More importantly, though, Schmitt's exceptional sovereign, like the God of traditional theism, must be both singular and personal. Insofar as liberal political theory attempts to minimize or even eliminate that form of political authority, it is not a politics at all. From liberalism there is only a short step to the extremes of anarchism, which Schmitt views as a malign form of antipolitics. Indeed, he dedicates the enigmatic final chapter of *Political Theology* to the political demonology of the reactionary Roman Catholic thinker Donoso Cortés, who opposed the demonic anarchism of his time and who clearly serves as a stand-in for Schmitt himself. Just as the attempt to do away with war leads to the worst possible war, so the attempt to do away with Godlike sovereign authority will lead to the sovereignty of the devil.[44]

What begins as a seemingly descriptive and methodological text concludes on a thinly veiled normative note. For Schmitt, the exceptional space of sovereignty is the foundation of the most important sphere of human action, the political, and that space must be occupied by a responsible human agent. While sovereignty is as ineradicable as the political itself, the tendency in liberal democracies is to deny this fact of human existence. This denial is not only delusional but will result in disaster—a nihilistic form of sovereignty propagating the worst and most inhuman war. From this dire diagnosis of his contemporary predicament, it is only a short distance to the calculation that installing some sovereign, *any* sovereign, is the only way to save the modern world from its own nihilism. And this calculation surely weighed heavily in Schmitt's disastrous decision to lend his formidable intellect to the service of Adolf Hitler. As so often happens, desperation to stave off the worst at any cost turned out to be the path toward the very worst.

From Restricted to General Political Theology

Virtually no exponents of political theology have wanted to follow Schmitt down that path. Indeed, just the opposite—as I noted above, Schmitt's theory has arguably enjoyed its greatest success on the political left. The reason such an unlikely affinity is possible is that this founding text of political theology is operating on two levels at once. On the one hand, there is the level on which two opposed senses of political theology—the theologization of the political in the sense of both carrying theological norms into the political realm and treating the political with a quasi-religious reverence—are at play in a mutually reinforcing way that makes them very difficult to untangle. Yet at the root of both, conceptually speaking, is the third sense of political theology: the study of the sheer fact of transfers between the two realms.

To attempt to separate out this more purely descriptive and analytic sense of political theology, I would like to return to the methodological passage I quoted above: "All significant concepts of the modern theory of the state are secularized theological concepts, not only because of their historical development—in which they were transferred from theology to the theory of the state, whereby, for example, the omnipotent God became the omnipotent lawgiver—but also because of their systematic structure, the recognition of which is necessary for a sociological consideration of these concepts."[45] In light of our discussion here, it should be clear that Schmitt is "front-loading" his conception of political theology to match his own normative commitments. There is a strong implication that the theology of which modern political theory is a secularized version should remain somehow normative, and this cashes out in the figure of the sovereign lawgiver, who is not only the privileged site of comparison between the political and the theological but is put forward as a virtual god on earth. As I have already discussed, most work in political theology has followed Schmitt's lead here by focusing on the question of sovereignty and the relationship between medieval Christendom and secular modernity.

Despite Schmitt's efforts to put his thumb on the scale, however, this passage has broader implications. If we break it down, his famous claim that "all significant concepts of the modern theory of the state are secularized theological concepts" rests on two pillars of support. The first is "their historical development"—a point that Schmitt strongly emphasizes with his parenthetical example, which brings the full weight of his preceding chapters to bear. Yet the second reason, "because of their systematic structure," is actually the more foundational claim. It is only because political and theological systems are similarly structured in the same historical moment that concepts can migrate between the two realms across history.

Schmitt's subsequent argument bears out this priority of the synchronic over the diachronic by focusing on the parallels between the mutually contemporary phenomena of deism and absolutist monarchy. This move not only deemphasizes the locus classicus of the transition from the medieval to the modern. It also shows that the "theology" in question here need not be a doctrinal theology tied to religious practices and institutions but could also embrace what Pascal might call the "god of the philosophers." In other words, the "theology" in political theology could be taken as embracing a whole range of metaphysical systems with no particular relationship to faith or historical revelation. Schmitt has his own reasons for choosing the historical moment he does—for him, it appears to represent the last gasp of the monotheistic model of sovereignty that he takes to be so essential—but for analysts unbound by those normative commitments, he implicitly (if unintentionally) opens the door to seeking homologies between political and metaphysical systems that are not structured along monotheistic lines.

In his elaboration of the curious phrase "sociology of concepts," Schmitt solidifies this priority of the synchronic by explaining why homologies between the two realms exist. In a passage that could almost be read as a preemptive rebuke to some of the more impressionistic versions of political theology, Schmitt says: "It is thus not a sociology of the concept of sovereignty when, for example, the monarchy of the seventeenth century is characterized as the real that is 'mirrored' in the Cartesian concept of God."[46]

The problem with this approach is that it is reductionistic, explaining away the metaphysical by reference to the political. By contrast, Schmitt wants to trace both modes of thought to a common root:

> But it is a sociology of the concept of sovereignty when the historical-political status of the monarchy of that epoch is shown to correspond to the general state of consciousness that was characteristic of western Europeans at that time, and when the juristic construction of the historical-political reality can find a concept whose structure is in accord with the structure of metaphysical concepts. . . . The metaphysical image that a definite epoch forges of the world has the same structure as what the world immediately understands to be appropriate as a form of its political organization.[47]

Both political and metaphysical thought, in other words, express the deep convictions of a particular community at a particular time and place about how the world is and ought to be. More than that, they both share a similar ambition to provide a coherent account for the whole range of human experience, and this shared drive toward systematicity and totality leads to the often uncanny homologies between the two fields that political theology aims to uncover.

In theological terms we could say that political theology deals with what Paul Tillich calls "the ultimate concern," a phrase that designates the reality that is most meaningful and grants meaning to everything else.[48] From the political side it would be an investigation of the sources of legitimacy, of the right of political authority to demand our obedience and loyalty. And here already, a potential transfer between the two realms immediately presents itself. Does not every political authority claim to be an ultimate concern, which in the last analysis can claim to override every other concern, even our concern for self-preservation? Coming from the other direction, one could characterize the discourse of theodicy as an attempt to vindicate God's right to be God, to demand our obedience and loyalty, in the face of our experience of suffering and evil. In other words, the theological problem of evil, the enduring existential anxiety over the question of how an omnipotent and benevolent God could allow anything but unalloyed good, is a version of the political problem of legitimacy. And to continue the exchange, this theological discourse often mobilizes techniques that could easily be transferred to political apologetics: blaming bad outcomes on an external enemy (most famously the devil) or arguing that respecting the freedom of God's subjects to make their own decisions is more important than guaranteeing positive results in every situation.[49]

No solution to the problem of evil or the problem of legitimacy can endure forever. Schmitt admits as much when he documents the transition from the metaphysical monotheism and political absolutism of early modernity toward "the elimination of all theistic and transcendental conceptions and the formation of a new concept of legitimacy" that culminates in the nineteenth century.[50] For Schmitt, the resulting paradigm is no political theology at all, but there seems to be no intrinsic reason to draw that conclusion. From the perspective of a sociology of concepts, there is a "new concept of legitimacy" emerging, which finds its metaphysical parallel in "a more or less clear immanence-pantheism or a positivist indifference toward any metaphysics," and in this context Hegel presents a compelling synthesis of political and metaphysical thought.[51] The "immanence-pantheism" Schmitt attributes to Hegel does not achieve total hegemony, but that is in keeping with Schmitt's own previous example, insofar as the Cartesian metaphysical theology of the early modern period also had to contend with a more radical empiricism—two trends that are both represented in the work of Hobbes, an exemplary figure for Schmitt.

I propose, then, that Schmitt gives us two visions of political theology in his foundational text. The first is the more restricted political theology grounded in his normative commitments to the political as the "ultimate concern" of human existence and to a singular, personal, omnipotent sovereign as the guarantor of the political. The second, of which the former would be only a narrow subset, is the most general concept of political theology—a nonreductionist analysis of the homologies between political and theological or metaphysical systems, grounded in the recognition that both types of systems are attempts to grapple with the perennial dilemma that is represented theologically as the problem of evil and politically as the problem of legitimacy.

Within this general framework a particular historical moment like the early modern period may serve as an especially clear example of the kinds of parallels political theology seeks to discern, but there are no particular grounds to view it as normative or superior nor to think that political theology is more suited to study that paradigm than the democratic, non-monotheistic one that succeeds it. Furthermore, a general political theology would recognize that while the political and the theological or metaphysical tend to converge toward the kinds of parallels evinced during those exemplary historical moments, there is no guarantee that a stable parallel will emerge in any given time and place. Finally, it will recognize that no approach to the problem of evil or the problem of legitimacy can claim to be definitive or permanent. Rather, every political-theological paradigm is continually menaced by unforeseen contingencies as well as unacknowledged internal contradictions—the very external enemies and internal crises that the Schmittian sovereign must grapple with.

Neoliberalism as a Political Theology

In terms of Schmitt's restricted version, neoliberalism could never qualify as a political-theological paradigm. In its subordination of the political to the economic, it would appear to be a delusional antipolitics at best and a demonic perversion of the political at worst. I want to emphasize this point: I am not claiming that neoliberalism is somehow a political-theological paradigm in the narrow Schmittian sense. Forging such a connection is neither necessary nor desirable. It is not the continued existence of sovereign state authority that makes neoliberalism a political theology in my view, for instance, nor do I base my claim on the theological roots of economic concepts as traced by Taylor, Agamben, and others.

Neoliberalism really does fall outside the purview of the restricted Schmittian political theology. And that is no accident, because as Foucault points out in *The Birth of Biopolitics*, neoliberalism arose in part as a reaction to the historical experience of totalitarianism. What Foucault characterizes as the "state phobia" of neoliberalism grows from two roots, both of which take the totalitarian state as the logical endpoint of state power: first, "the idea that the state possesses in itself and through its own dynamism a sort of power of expansion, an intrinsic tendency to expand" and, second, the idea that all the various types of states represent "the successive branches of one and the same great tree of state control in its continuous and unified expansion."[52] One can certainly make the case, as Foucault does, that this view of the state is simplistic and one-sided. Be that as it may, it could not be more clear that the Schmittian quasi deification of the state as the highest principle of human existence is utterly anathema to the neoliberal project. It is precisely what neoliberalism aims to prevent.

Yet despite its diametrical opposition to the narrow version of Schmitt's project, neoliberalism can nonetheless be understood as a political theology in the more general sense. Under neoliberalism, a set of core convictions about how the world is and ought to be—what Friedman calls "the underlying current of opinion"—informs both a theory of governance and a theory of human nature, meaning that neoliberalism represents an account of the sources of legitimacy for our social institutions and of the moral order of the world. From this perspective, the fact that its account is opposed to that of the restricted Schmittian political theology supports rather than detracts from its claim to be a political theology. Competition and rivalry are only possible between peers—in this case, two approaches to the problem of political theology, both operating at the same level of totality.

I assume that for some, however, the root difficulty in viewing neoliberalism as a political theology does not stem from an unwillingness to broaden the latter concept but from a sense that it is inappropriate to view neoliberalism in such grandiose terms. As I have noted before, most popular conceptions of neoliberalism boil down to a libertarian polemic against the state, grounded in an exaggerated confidence in the market to solve all problems (if only we could stop interfering with it). And it is striking how seldom neoliberal policy delivers the promised results. Even the greatest successes are a disappointment.

To choose arguably the most high-profile recent example, Obamacare is so complex that even those who benefit from it often fail to grasp that fact. The net result of its convoluted approach is that the United States continues to spend vastly more per capita on health care than the rest of the developed world while still falling short of universal coverage. Indeed, as the Republicans were moving to dismantle the program in early 2017, Democrats seized on a well-timed success story: as a result of Obamacare, the percentage of uninsured Americans had fallen below 10 percent. I do not wish to downplay the benefits of expanded health care access, which for many individuals is quite literally a matter of life and death. But that very fact only highlights the absurdity of exulting in the triumph that "only" around one in ten Americans lacks that access.

Within the general context of neoliberal policy making, however, Obamacare does represent something of an outlier: it aims to solve a clear problem (Americans lack reliable access to health care) by a fairly direct route (making it easier to obtain health insurance). Many neoliberal approaches are neither as targeted nor as successful. Broadly speaking, the privatization of government services has not increased their quality or reduced their cost. The promise that greater reliance on market mechanisms would lead to less bureaucracy has proven false, as Mark Fisher has forcefully demonstrated in *Capitalist Realism*. Reducing taxes on the wealthy has not led to more beneficial investment and greater prosperity. Instead, growth rates in the neoliberal era have consistently failed to reach the levels associated with Fordism even as income and wealth inequality have skyrocketed. And free trade has destroyed livelihoods and communities in many former industrial areas while any benefits it provides are indirect and largely invisible.

Overall, increasing inequality appears to be the most consistent outcome of neoliberalism. Tax cuts allow the wealthy to amass greater fortunes, while contributing to inequality in less direct ways as well. For instance, when the top tax rate was 90 percent or more, as it was for most of the postwar era in the United States, there was little benefit to increasing an individual's pay above that threshold, given that the vast majority of the added salary would go toward taxes—better to reinvest that money in the company and its workers. Similarly, high taxes on capital gains virtually mandate a longer-term perspective on investment, since cashing in too quickly would result in losing a greater portion of the profits to taxation. By contrast, in a low-tax regime both management and shareholders (who are often the same individuals, because of stock-based compensation of executives) are emboldened to extract as much short-term profit out of a company as possible, at the expense of workers as well as the firm's long-term prospects. Similarly, privatization provides opportunities for individuals and firms to extract profit out of essential public services, while free trade has functioned to increase corporate profitability by allowing firms to seek out the cheapest possible labor force.

In this context David Harvey's move to treat increasing inequality as the true identifying trait of neoliberalism and to dismiss the ideological trappings as mere window dressing for a generation-long cash grab by the capitalist class appears quite plausible. And it would certainly be naive not to recognize that this compatibility with the interests of the capitalist class is one major factor in why neoliberalism emerged as the hegemonic "solution" to the breakdown of the Fordist order and has retained that status despite its very evident failures. Even if we concede that income inequality has contributed to the power of the neoliberal order, however, we can hardly regard it as a source of the regime's legitimacy. After all, it is difficult to imagine anyone voluntarily submitting to a social order that openly promises to enrich the already wealthy at the expense of the rest of the population. And experience bears out this intuition: out-of-control inequality is arguably the single greatest factor in the ongoing decline of neoliberalism's legitimacy worldwide.

The lens of political theology helps us to see that neoliberalism is precisely a theory of legitimacy. Foucault had already recognized as much in *The Birth of Biopolitics*. Summarizing and expanding on the work of the German theorist Ludwig Erhard, he claims that the underlying goal of neoliberalism differs from traditional accounts of law and sovereignty in that it envisions a new form of the state that functions "not to constrain, but simply to create a space of freedom, to guarantee a freedom, and precisely to guarantee it in the economic domain."[53] Under such a regime, "any number of individuals freely agree to play this game of economic freedom guaranteed by the institutional framework," and this would be the basis for their "adherence to this framework": "it would imply that consent has been given to any decision that may be taken to guarantee this economic freedom or to secure that which makes this economic freedom possible. In other words, the institution of economic freedom will have to function, or at any rate will be able to function as a siphon, as it were, as a point of attraction from the formation of a political sovereignty."[54]

One could claim that Erhard's approach is a special case, arising as it did in postwar Germany, where a divided nation and a conquered state made it necessary to find a new principle of legitimacy for the political order. Yet Foucault argues that it would be a mistake to view these early beginnings of German neoliberalism as "a pure and simple calculation of political groups or political personnel of Germany after its defeat":

It is something other than a political calculation, even if it is completely per-
meated by political calculation. No more is it an ideology, although, of course,
there is a whole set of perfectly coherent ideas, analytical principles, and so
forth. What is involved in fact is a new programming of liberal governmentality. It is an internal reorganization that, once again, does not ask the state
what freedom it will leave to the economy, but asks the economy how its
freedom can have a state-creating function and role, in the sense that it will
really make possible the foundation of the state's legitimacy.[55]

Making all due allowance for the complex intellectual genealogy Foucault traces
here, I would argue that this is the core strategy of all forms of neoliberalism:
founding the legitimacy of the political order on the guarantee of economic freedom. And this move is plausible because of an account of human nature wherein
freedom is best expressed through economic exchange and competition and is
continually menaced by extraeconomic forces such as the state.

     To put it in my terms, the political theology of neoliberalism is grounded
in freedom as its ultimate concern. On the theological or metaphysical side,
it sets up participation in economic competition as the highest expression of
human personhood, which leads directly to its account of what is permissible
in the political realm. There is of course much to object to in this neoliberal
political theology. From the perspective of traditional political theory (including conventional political theology), its economic grounding of politics
represents a short circuit, and its vision of freedom is extremely narrow. The
next two chapters will discuss both of these issues in turn, but for now, I want
to draw attention to how tightly integrated neoliberalism is as a political
theology—so much so that it can be difficult to separate out the political and
"theological" elements.

     The very simplicity of its approach lends it a remarkable coherence that
can be seen in all the major policy goals of neoliberalism. Globalization and
free trade tame the state, subjecting it to economic discipline on the world
stage in a way that helps prevent it from infringing on economic freedom.
Privatization expands the economic model into social services, allowing the
state to "shop" for the best service providers. Though the state is constrained
in some ways (by limiting taxation and regulatory authority), it is in other
ways very active in the work of cultivating, supporting, and even creating

markets—as when Obamacare effectively created a market in individual health insurance plans, an area where the market was previously so dysfunctional as to be essentially nonexistent.

The example of Obamacare also highlights the peculiar nature of neoliberal freedom. One of its most controversial provisions was a mandate that all Americans must have health insurance coverage. From a purely libertarian perspective, this is an impermissible infringement on economic freedom— surely if I am free to make my own economic decisions, I am also free to choose not to purchase health insurance. Yet the mandate fits perfectly with the overall ethos of neoliberalism. On a practical level this aspect of the plan was a necessary complement to the rule forbidding insurers from rejecting applicants with a preexisting medical condition, which would allow people to wait until they were sick to purchase insurance, leading to a collapse of the market by either bankrupting insurers or leading to out-of-control premium increases. In this respect the mandate represented the state's attempt to set up and preserve a functioning market in individual health insurance plans. At the same time, it expressed a deeper truth of neoliberalism. Within the market created by Obamacare, I was free to choose whichever health plan I might want, but I was not free to opt out of the market altogether. If I am not inclined to express my economic freedom in that sphere, then I must be forced to be free.

This same logic of constraint appears throughout neoliberalism at every level. At the global scale, if states attempt to "opt out" of the neoliberal order, they will lose out on investment and jobs as companies move to more compliant (or, to use the term of art, "competitive") countries. On the individual level there is an even harder constraint: the sheer necessity for survival. Though even neoliberals recognize the need for some base-level protection against abject poverty, the social safety net is set up to "incentivize" work as much as possible. Meanwhile, the erosion of job security through deunionization and other measures to maximize "flexibility" in labor markets means that workers are forced into a perpetual competition. Even when they succeed in finding a steady job, they have to fight continually to keep it. And in between, at the level of the individual firm, deregulation on the governmental level does not mean companies can simply do whatever they want. Instead, they are subjected to the more comprehensive and inescapable constraint of market discipline. If we ask why a particular company cannot choose to treat its workers better and offer them job security (in the hopes of better productivity, for instance), the answer is that the market would never allow it: a shareholder revolt or hostile takeover would lead to the removal of any management team that made such a scandalous proposal.

Overall, then, in neoliberalism an account of human nature where economic competition is the highest value leads to a political theory where the prime duty of the state is to enable, and indeed mandate, such competition, and the result is a world wherein individuals, firms, and states are all continually constrained to express themselves via economic competition. This means that neoliberalism tends to create a world in which neoliberalism is "true." A more coherent and self-reinforcing political theology can scarcely be imagined—but that, I will argue, is precisely what any attempt to create an alternative to neoliberalism must do.

CHAPTER 2

THE POLITICAL AND THE ECONOMIC

Thus far, I have distinguished two forms of political theology at work in Schmitt's foundational text. The first is a restricted form focused on sovereignty and the transition from the medieval to the modern, which has largely set the agenda for research in the field. The second is a more general form of which the restricted form is only a narrow subset, which would study the parallels between political and theological or metaphysical discourse as rooted in the interminable struggle with what can be variously called the problem of evil or the problem of legitimacy. I have also provided a broad overview of what it would mean to view neoliberalism as a political-theological paradigm in the broader sense and some initial indication of the advantages such an approach might have over the dominant Marxist and Foucauldian interpretations of neoliberalism.

At the same time, I have identified a major obstacle to any attempt to view neoliberalism through a political-theological lens: the field's deeply polemical relationship to the economic realm. My task in this chapter will be to show that this bias against the economic, just like the bias in favor of sovereignty and medieval-to-modern genealogies, is an arbitrary one that leads the field into unnecessary contradictions and aporias. At bottom, my argument is based on my conviction that one of the most attractive things about political theology is the way it overcomes—or, perhaps more accurately, shows a principled disregard for—simplistic binaries. In connection

with the political-economic binary in particular, a political-theological account promises a nonreductionist account of the role of economics in the
neoliberal order.

If all I wanted was a theoretical apparatus for interpreting the economic
dynamics of the neoliberal order, of course, I should look no further than
Marxism. David Harvey's influential account is a case in point: virtually no
other interpreters of neoliberalism show anywhere near the same confidence
and rigor in their handling of economic material. At the same time, I have
already pointed out that Harvey seems to have difficulty specifying what is
unique about neoliberalism. His Marxist approach leads him to view political
institutions and ideology as superstructures that ultimately only reflect the
more fundamental economic base or mode of production—but once we leave
aside neoliberalism's explicit ideology and political ambitions, what is left but
the same old story of capitalism? In Dardot and Laval's words, "Trapped in a
conception that makes the 'logic of capital' an autonomous motor of history,
[Marxists] reduce the latter to the sheer repetition of the same scenarios,
with the same characters in new costumes and the same plots in new settings."[1] This economic reductionism "presupposes that the 'bourgeoisie' is an
historical subject which persists over time; that it pre-exists the relations of
struggle it engages in with other classes; and that it was sufficient for it to
apprise, influence, and corrupt politicians for them to abandon Keynesian
policies and compromise formulas between labor and capital."[2] Such a simplistic narrative is belied by Harvey's own "recognition of the fact that classes
have been profoundly changed during the process of neo-liberalization"—
meaning that the beneficiaries cannot have planned the neoliberal push in
any straightforward way.[3] More than that, an economic-reductionist account
ignores the decisive role of the state in the development of the neoliberal
order: "To believe that 'financial markets' one fine day eluded the grasp of
politics is nothing but a fairy tale. It was states, and global economic organi-
zations, in close collusion with private actors, that fashioned rules conducive
to the expansion of market finance."[4] In other words, politics are not epiphenomenal to economic structures but directly transform them.

Dardot and Laval are far from the first to notice a problem here. Marxists have always had an ambivalent relationship with the tendency toward
economic reductionism in their intellectual tradition, by turns embracing it

as the only possible basis for a scientific Marxism and distancing themselves from its more extreme implications. The most popular version of the latter strategy can be encapsulated in the notion that the economy is "determinative in the last instance," which seems to provide some breathing room for a relative autonomy of the political-ideological "superstructure" over and against the economic-material "base." As Ernesto Laclau and Chantal Mouffe argue, however, such a threading of the needle ultimately fails: if the economy is determinative in the last instance, it is *always* determinative.[5]

Working in the wake of Laclau and Mouffe's intervention, Slavoj Žižek has reconceived the material "base" more abstractly as the existence of an insoluble deadlock or obstacle that Jacques Lacan designated as "the Real." On this basis Žižek puts forth a new vision of Marxism in which ideology critique took on an unexpectedly central role as a Hegelian critique of the Marxist tradition allowed him to move past conventional reductionism.[6] Žižek has proven to be a helpful interlocutor for many working in political theology (including Eric Santner and myself),[7] and that dialogue has been reciprocal insofar as Žižek has engaged extensively with theological themes in many of his writings. Yet his attempt at a synthesis of Hegel and Lacan (two thinkers who are surely already complex enough on their own) has grown more and more self-referential and unresponsive to changing political and economic realities.[8] If this increasingly baroque—and still incomplete—system is what it takes to overcome Marxist reductionism, why not simply start from the nonreductionist standpoint of political theology?

Here I may seem to be knocking at an open door, however, insofar as Foucauldianism already represents a nonreductionist approach to the interplay of discursive, political, and economic forces. Foucault starts from the position that both knowledge and institutional practices contribute equally to networks of power, and in contrast to conventional political theology's animus against the economic, he includes economic practices and techniques alongside the many other modes in which power is exercised.

With respect to the political-economic dyad that is my quarry in this chapter, then, Foucauldianism provides a model for my general theory of political theology. In the next chapter, I hope to demonstrate that political theology's focus on the sources of legitimacy—which carries with it a focus on moral agency, responsibility, and obligation—can help supplement the

Foucauldian account of neoliberalism by exposing the way that neoliberalism presents itself as a moral order of the world and "hooks" us by exploiting our moral intuitions.

My first step down that path will be a consideration of Wendy Brown's *Undoing the Demos*, which attempts to combine a Foucauldian analysis with an account of popular sovereignty in order to hold open the hope of overcoming neoliberalism. In this respect Brown is already pushing Foucault toward something very much like political theology, but she does so at the cost of reaffirming the very political-economic binary I am seeking to overcome. After analyzing the disadvantages of this binary for Brown's project, I will trace the roots of her approach in Arendt. I will then turn to two contemporary thinkers, Giorgio Agamben and Dotan Leshem, who both attempt, in their own ways, to investigate the relationship between the political and the economic by means of a synthesis of Arendt and Foucault and who both end up in similar deadlocks as Brown. Having established that the political-economic dyad that I call "Arendt's axiom" leads to a dead end, I will take up a variety of alternative proposals that seem to me to point toward the possibility of a political theology that operates outside that misleading binary. Finally, I will conclude the chapter by arguing that there is actually no stable political-economic binary but rather that it serves as a kind of "container" for a series of more fundamental binaries that different political-theological paradigms sort out and combine in different ways.

Demonizing Neoliberalism

In the lectures collected under the title *The Birth of Biopolitics*, Foucault, writing at a time when neoliberalism was just starting to cohere into a governing rationality, approaches the topic with some equanimity and even fascination. In fact, though most Foucauldians have used these lectures as the starting point for a harsh critique of the neoliberal order, some commentators have detected in Foucault's stance a deep sympathy for neoliberalism as an alternative to the apparatuses of control represented by the welfare state.[9]

Future scholars will detect no such ambiguity in Wendy Brown's *Undoing the Demos*. Writing not only amid the wreckage of the Global Financial Crisis but as a witness to neoliberalism's shockingly rapid reconsolidation of power in the wake of that catastrophe, Brown evinces not even the most grudging appreciation of the mechanisms of neoliberal hegemony. A voice crying out in the wilderness, Brown wants her readers to recognize the profound danger that neoliberalism represents. This danger is bigger than any of the well-known features of the neoliberal agenda: the erosion of welfare protections, the ever-accelerating income inequality, and so forth. Though she does not explicitly use the term, one is tempted to claim that she is pointing to an *ontological* danger—the danger that a crucial part of what we have come to regard as human nature might be permanently eclipsed. Specifically, neoliberalism threatens to undo our sense that human beings are creatures who can collectively rule themselves, and more insidiously still, to make us forget that we ever could have *wanted* to do something so improbable.

Brown situates her project of resistance very explicitly in terms of the political-economic binary. In the opening of her first chapter she defines her investigation as "a theoretical consideration of the ways that neoliberalism, a peculiar form of reason that configures all aspects of existence in economic terms, is quietly undoing basic elements of democracy . . . converting the distinctly *political* character, meaning, and operation of democracy's constituent elements into *economic* ones."[10] In defining this distinction, which structures her entire argument, she draws on the authority of Aristotle, Marx, and Arendt, all of whom, in her account, align the economic with servitude and the political with freedom. Hence, with its one-sided emphasis on the economic to the exclusion of any other concern, neoliberalism limits human aspiration to "the limited form of human existence that Aristotle and later Hannah Arendt designated as 'mere life' and that Marx called life 'confined by necessity.' . . . Neoliberal rationality eliminates what these thinkers term 'the good life' (Aristotle) or 'the true realm of freedom' (Marx), by which they did not mean luxury, leisure, or indulgence, but rather the cultivation and expression of distinctly human capacities for ethical and political freedom, creativity, unbounded reflection, or invention" (43). In Brown's account, her three authorities (joined now by John Stuart Mill) believe that "the potential of the human species is realized not through, but beyond the struggle for existence and wealth accumulation" (43). In the terms of neoliberalism's economic reconfiguration of the human prospect, however, "there are no motivations, drives, or aspirations apart from economic ones, [and] there is nothing to being human apart from 'mere life'" (44).

Brown identifies two major institutions in the modern West that have cultivated the space of authentic human freedom that she calls the political: the liberal-democratic state and liberal arts education. Though she acknowledges the profound failings of both, she views them as promising insofar as they keep alive the desire for real freedom, even in their very inadequacy. By contrast, the neoliberal takeover of political and educational institutions removes that aspiration even as a point of reference. Whatever remains of democratic rhetoric is hollowed out into neoliberal buzzwords—consent of the governed becomes stakeholder buy-in, public policy is reduced to the implementation of "best practices," etc.—and education's promise of self-cultivation and personal growth is replaced by the endless accumulation of human capital.

Hence Brown would disagree with Schmitt that "politics cannot be exterminated."[11] The danger she is warning against is precisely that the process of exterminating it is well under way. Yet in other respects there is in Brown's account a striking resemblance to Schmitt's concept of the political. Most notably, both Brown and Schmitt agree that the political represents the highest sphere of human existence. It is a sphere that has to do with rule—popular sovereignty for Brown, dictatorial sovereignty for Schmitt—and also with dispute. With her democratic perspective, Brown is not explicitly concerned with anything like Schmitt's friend-enemy distinction but rather with the necessary conflict of democratic politics, which is based on the general principle that the given order of things must always be open to challenge and transformation according to the will of the people.

It is here that a deeper resonance with Schmitt's concept of the political begins to emerge. I have already noted that Brown is well aware of the failings of actual existing democratic institutions. Most galling of all, one assumes, is the fact that, at least in the major Western countries, neoliberalism was implemented by means of nominally democratic processes. A common rhetorical trope for defenders of democracy is to take the position that democracy cannot fail, it can only be failed—hence if democracy delivers a bad result, it is because the decision-making process was insufficiently democratic. Brown does not take this route. She openly acknowledges that democracy, as "political self-rule by the people, whoever the people are" (20), offers no guarantee of good outcomes. For Brown, "democracy is neither a panacea nor a complete form of political life" (210). It must depend on the support of good institutions and education, though even here there are no guarantees because of "Rousseau's paradox: to support good institutions, the people must be antecedently what only good institutions can make them" (200). In the end there is no positive, substantive reason to prefer democracy, only the claim that if we lose it, "we lose the language and frame by which we are accountable to the present and entitled to make our own future, the language and frame with which we might contest the forces otherwise claim-ing that future" (210).

This defense of democracy is, if anything, even more openly tautological than Schmitt's defense of the political: we should preserve democracy as a space of contestation because otherwise we will lose democracy as a space of contestation. If we might ask what, precisely, we are contesting, then only one answer is possible: neoliberalism as a purely economic antipolitics. Here once again we are edging into Schmitt's territory, as Brown seems to be proposing a kind of metapolitical version of the friend-enemy distinction, a struggle between the political as such and that which threatens the political "way of life," namely the economic. And in the end she even follows Schmitt's lead in theologizing this struggle, setting up neoliberal economism as a false god with a "perverse theology of markets" (221) and an implacable demand for human sacrifice on the idolatrous altars of GDP and global competitiveness (216–19).

Alongside these (presumably unintentional) parallels, there is a deeper resonance with the political-theological project of tracing governing para-digms to the deep convictions of a given age. More specifically, Brown traces the root of the neoliberal paradigm to what she calls "civilizational despair": "At the triumphal 'end of history' in the West, most have ceased to believe in the human capacity to craft and sustain a world that is humane, free, sustain-able, and, above all, modestly under human control. . . . Ceding all power to craft the future to markets, it insists that markets 'know best'" (221). Yet this is more like a negative political theology, because it correlates a lack of positive conviction (despair) with a lack of any political order or project (neoliberalism). This account of the rise of neoliberalism is exactly parallel to Schmitt's account of the rise of classical liberalism. For Brown, the ideal is the good old days of Fordism rather than the good old days of early modern absolutism, but the structure is the same: for Brown as for Schmitt, the era that came after their respective ideals did not put forth a new and different political paradigm, but sowed the seeds for a demonic antipolitics. In the face of such an implacable foe, the only answer is to assert the necessity of the political as such—before it is too late.

Thus, even if Brown does not explicitly use the term, she is explicitly pushing the Foucauldian account of neoliberalism in the direction of political theology—and from my perspective, in so doing she loses what is most appealing about the Foucauldian analysis and inadvertently takes up what is most dangerous in conventional political theology. Even from a purely Foucauldian perspective, her reading of neoliberalism is questionable insofar as it is premised on a distinction between *homo politicus* and *homo oeconomicus* that Foucault does not ignore or downplay (as Brown claims) but explicitly rejects. In the Foucauldian account, economic and liberal-democratic means are both intertwined in the broader ensemble of governmental techniques that define the modern era. Insisting on a clear distinction, much less a rivalry, between the two models is not a supplement to Foucault's analysis but a break with it.

Meanwhile, the concept of the political in Brown's terms is so underspecified that her break with Foucault brings no clear benefit. This supposedly highest realm of human existence amounts, in the end, to the maintenance of the very possibility of resistance against neoliberalism—as though such resistance is not already happening all the time. In her demonization of neoliberalism she exaggerates its power, imagining that the most distant dreams of neoliberal ideologues are virtually a *fait accompli*, and the narrow window of political resistance is closing. And her vision of political resistance is almost entirely negative and backward-looking, focused on what we have lost in the transition from Fordism. Those losses are real and devastating, but Brown risks indulging in a nostalgia that can only imagine rebuilding the very institutions that neoliberalism has already proven itself quite capable of destroying.

A helpful alternative here is Jodi Dean's *Crowds and Party*.[12] In contrast to the despair over the loss of political resistance that Brown at once diagnoses and participates in, Dean presupposes the existence of a radical political potential in the resistance movements that have erupted continually throughout the neoliberal era. The task of activists and political theorists is to take the demand for transformation embodied in movements like Occupy and Black Lives Matter and help them formulate concrete programs and take on durable institutional forms. While her hope for a return to the party form could be seen as its own form of nostalgia, it is clear that Dean has in mind a renewed vision of the party that can take into account both the failures and the real successes of past movements in the course of building an institutional structure that can respond to the radically different circumstances we face in the present.

Indeed, from the perspective of Dean's *Democracy and Other Neoliberal Fantasies*, Brown ironically takes up a number of positions that could be viewed as distinctively neoliberal: fetishizing a concept of democracy that turns out to have little concrete content, echoing the apocalyptic rhetoric that Dean shows to fall easily off the tongues of American presidents in the neoliberal era, and arguably indulging in a paranoia about neoliberalism's successes that resonates with the growing prominence of conspiracy theories in contemporary politics.[13] The last point is most striking given the political context of Brown's book: writing as the American neoliberal regime continued to descend into economic stagnation and political deadlock and only a few short years before energetic challenges to the neoliberal status quo erupted in both major parties, Brown nevertheless treats neoliberalism's final victory as all but assured. Overall, what Dean says of the American left's reaction to George W. Bush's 2000 Electoral College victory could be repurposed as a critique of Brown's relationship to neoliberalism: "It's almost as if we believed in their strength and unity, their power and influence, more than they did themselves."[14]

Enclosing the Economic

How do we get from Brown's full-throated opposition to the neoliberal order to a seeming essentialization of neoliberalism that even echoes some of neoliberalism's key rhetorical tropes? I would argue that the seeds of this unhappy result are already present in the very weapon she levels against the neoliberal order: the political-economic dyad. While her goal in deploying this binary is to keep open the space for political opposition to the neoliberal order, it has the side-effect of identifying neoliberalism with a purportedly invariant structure of human experience. This move tilts the scales in advance so that any outcome but the total and final victory of neoliberalism seems almost impossible to imagine.

To flesh out this claim, it is helpful to turn to Brown's primary authorities: Aristotle, Marx, and Arendt. For Brown, while all three recognize that the economic provides the foundation for our biological survival, they are unanimous in privileging a sphere of life beyond the economic where the fullness of humanity (the "good life") is to be found, a sphere called the political. As a reading of Aristotle and Arendt, this seems plausible enough, but it is difficult to understand why Brown is invoking Marx as an authority in this context. Surely Marx looks forward to something like the Aristotelian "good life," but it makes little sense to identify that "good life" with "the political." If anything, the "good life" of communism comes after the end of what humanity has known as the political—namely, class struggle. More than that, the development of the economic sphere does not imperil but enables the emergence of the postpolitical "good life," which is premised on a material abundance so great that conflicts over scarce resources and coercion of labor will no longer be necessary. Doubtless Marx anticipates that development and transformation will continue and that it will be collectively self-directed, but the notion of "the political" as a space of contestation seems an odd fit. And in the meantime political struggle is directed at gaining as much control as possible over the production process and ultimately the productive apparatus itself; in other words, politics is subordinate to economic goals. It is certainly not the realm of the most authentic human self-actualization, which for Marx is found in the creative act of production—that is, once again in what Brown would see as the economic sphere.

Even this counterreading of Marx may seem artificial, however. Surely it makes more sense to say that Marx is aiming at a world in which something like the political-economic dyad would no longer obtain, where "the economic" would no longer exist as a realm of constraint and necessity and "the political" as a sphere of struggle and contestation would no longer be needed, at least not in the same way it is now. Brown's terms are simply not a good fit here, and her attempt to force Marx into them arouses the suspicion that she is primarily concerned with recruiting Marx's authority to shore up the left-wing credentials of a project for which Marx is not actually a major inspiration.

Far more foundational for Brown's argument is Aristotle's *Politics*, the first book of which discusses the household (*oikos*) and its management (*oikonomia*, the root of our "economy") in relation to the city (*polis*, hence "politics"). This choice is odd from several perspectives. First, it is unclear why an ancient Greek text should provide guidance for a model of political life that Brown mostly associates with modern liberal-democratic states. Second, and more substantively, it is unclear why a normative philosophical treatise from a slaveholding society provides us with any particular leverage for critiquing systems of domination.

This latter concern is particularly grave when we recognize that Brown is taking the masters from that slaveholding society as the normative models of human agency. This is most striking in her chapter on liberal arts education, where references to Marx fall aside entirely in favor of a near-exclusive reliance on Aristotle's authority. Tracing the origin of the phrase "liberal arts," Brown notes:

> Even in classical antiquity, the liberal arts (rooted in *liberus*, the Latin word for individual freedom) denoted the education appropriate to free men, in contrast to that of slaves. A liberal arts education, in other words, was necessary for free men to know and engage the world sufficiently to exercise that freedom. It was the knowledge that enabled the use of freedom, but that in an important sense also made men free insofar as it lifted them from the immediate present to a longer temporal and larger spatial domain, one accessible only through knowledge. (184)

She then goes on to characterize the midcentury achievement of "extending liberal arts education from the elite to the many" as "nothing short of a radical democratic event, one in which all became potentially eligible for the life of freedom long reserved for the few" (185). Here we might ask whether the attempt to deploy the style of education developed in a highly stratified, slave-owning society for the purposes of democratic equality is coherent or sustainable. Admittedly, as with her very guarded praise of actual existing liberal-democratic states, she is more interested in the aspiration opened up by mass higher education than in its obvious limits. Yet she seems not to recognize that the very structure of this educational program leads much more directly to something like the neoliberal project of creating a more inclusive elite rather than undercutting elitism, an agenda that fits well with the neoliberal trope of equality of opportunity as a substitute for equality of outcome. In other words, there may be a reason that higher education has proven to be ground zero for neoliberalization in most Western countries.

What is more troubling is her one-sided focus on the middle class, as in her lament that "we are no longer governed by the idea that upward mobility and middle-class status require schooling in the liberal arts" (182). This is a puzzling claim, because during the heyday of Fordism, middle-class status emphatically did not necessarily entail a liberal arts education. Americans remember that era as a golden age because the average high school–educated laborer, thanks to strong unions and supportive government policies, could reasonably expect all the comforts and privileges of middle-class life. Middle-class families in that era may have sent their children to college in the expectation of further social mobility, but vocational training—which Brown implicitly treats as a degrading pursuit—was a potential path into a well-remunerated unionized trade, and thereby into the middle class as well. The meritocratic credentialism that makes a college education the baseline condition of a financially stable, comfortable life is a product of the neoliberal era, not a casualty of it.

This distortion in Brown's view of the Fordist era arguably stems from the real root source of the political-economic binary around which she structures her work: Hannah Arendt's *The Human Condition*.[15] Published in 1958, a time when the Fordist project was not only a living reality but a relatively new one, Arendt's account of human nature and its vicissitudes evinces a palpable disdain for the burgeoning mass middle class and its consumer culture. This polemical purpose shapes her idiosyncratic reading of Aristotle, which bifurcates the household and the *polis* in an exaggerated way and poses the latter as a purely human creation over against the merely "natural" life of the household.[16]

This bias shows forth more clearly in Arendt's term for the type of human existence that is focused on the nonproductive labor associated with slaves: *animal laborans*. Aristotle, by contrast, never reduces the slave to the status of an animal, as shown in a passage where he wonders whether there is a virtue specific to slavery. This is a difficult question insofar as "there is an impasse either way, since, if there are virtues, in what respect do they differ from free people? And if there are not, that would be strange, since they are human beings and have a share in reason."[17] While his answer to the question is certainly unsatisfying from a modern perspective—"it is clear that [the slave] too needs a little virtue, enough that he does not fall short in his tasks on account of dissipation or cowardice"[18]—his insistence on the humanity of the slave is clear in his conclusion that "people are not speaking beautifully who deprive slaves of reason."[19] We are forced to conclude that in this respect, Arendt is among those who do not speak beautifully.

The same critique could be leveled at her bifurcation of the household from the *polis*. While Aristotle obviously does distinguish the two, it is not a matter of a binary opposition but of a continuum that leads from the household to the *polis*. On the very first page of the *Politics*, Aristotle takes issue with those who claim that the forms of rule present in the household and the city are simply the same, but his purpose is not to claim that the former are foreign or opposed to the latter. If that were the case, why would an account of the household belong in the *Politics* at all? Rather, the forms of rule found in the household represent the "beginnings" from which the human community grows,[20] through the intermediary step of the village as a collection of related households, until it becomes a city when, "so to speak, it gets to the threshold of self-sufficiency, coming into being for the sake of living, but being for the sake of living well."[21] What makes human beings unique is not simply political life but rather speech, which is "for disclosing what is just and what is unjust." And speech obviously takes place in both the city and the household, making both into sites of moral aspiration: "For this is distinctive of human beings in relation to the other animals, to be alone in having a perception of good and bad, just and unjust, and the rest, and it is an association involving these things that makes a household and a city."[22] The city plays a special role as the most fully developed form of human association in Aristotle's view, the whole without which the more partial forms of community cannot be fully understood. Yet simply because those forms are not fully developed does not mean that they are not fully human. Adriel Trott puts it well: "Aristotle's account does not depend on the severe division between an animal life focused on and limited by necessities and a political and free life. Life is always a way of life for Aristotle. Human beings are always already concerned with not just living, but living well."[23]

As a reading of Aristotle, then, Arendt's political-economic binary is re-ductive and even misleading, more revealing of her own polemical purpose in *The Human Condition* than of Aristotle's concepts and goals. Though other influential thinkers embrace a similar distinction (most notably for our pur-poses, Carl Schmitt), it is Arendt who most explicitly formulated it, and it is Arendt's authority that most often grounds its use in later works (such as Brown's). Hence, as I prepare to turn to two other recent works of political theology (or economic theology) that are structured around it, I propose that we designate the view that the political and economic realms are qualitatively distinct in a way that implies a normative hierarchical relationship between the two as "Arendt's axiom."

Arendt, Economy, and Theology

One of the greatest political theologians of our day, Giorgio Agamben, in-directly expresses his debt to Hannah Arendt from the very first sentences of *Homo Sacer*: "The Greeks had no single term to express what we mean by the word 'life.' They used two terms that, although traceable to a com-mon etymological root, are semantically and morphologically distinct: *zōē*, which expressed the simple fact of living common to all living beings (ani-mals, men, or gods), and *bios*, which indicated the way of living proper to an individual or a group."[24] This distinction has prompted considerable criti-cism, most notably from Jacques Derrida, who argues that the hard-and-fast division Agamben seems to posit is not supported by the textual evidence.[25] Whatever its basis in the ancient Greek corpus, however, its source as a phil-osophical argument is obvious: Arendt's *Human Condition*, where she makes a strikingly similar claim: "The word 'life,' however, has an altogether differ-ent meaning if it is related to the [distinctively human] world. . . . The chief characteristic of this specifically human life, whose appearance and disap-pearance constitute worldly events, is that it is itself always full of events which ultimately can be told as a story, establish a biography; it is of this life, *bios* as distinguished from mere *zōē*, that Aristotle said that it is 'some-how a kind of *praxis*'" (97). Agamben makes this connection explicit when he proclaims his intention to combine Foucault's theory of biopolitics with Arendt's analysis in *The Human Condition* of "the process that brings *homo laborans* [*sic*]—and, with it, biological life as such—gradually to occupy the very center of the political scene of modernity."[26] He is referring here to Arendt's narrative of the gradual eclipse of classical distinction between the political and the economic in favor of what she calls "the social," a realm in which the two fields collapse. His hope is that, by bringing Foucault's concept of biopolitics to bear on Arendt's concepts, he can build a connection between Arendt's "research in *The Human Condition* and the penetrating analyses she had previously devoted to totalitarian power (in which a biopolitical perspective is altogether lacking)" and at the same time fill in the lacuna in Foucault's analysis, which "never dwelt on the exemplary places of modern biopolitics: the concentration camp and the structure of the great totalitarian states of the twentieth century."[27]

Broadly speaking, then, though his ambitions are much broader, Agamben's project is structurally homologous to Brown's insofar as both attempt to supplement Foucault with Arendt. More than that, though they focus on different destructive regimes (concentration camps and neoliberalism, respectively), both trace their baleful effects to the collapse in the distinction between political and economic life, or in Arendt and Agamben's terms (if not Aristotle's), *bios* and *zōē*. In Agamben's analysis this collapse leaves the human being in the condition of *homo sacer*, the readily victimizable "bare life" that finds its exemplary form in the inmates of the Nazi concentration camps. While Brown is not prepared to attribute such a danger directly to the neoliberal program (which for her requires but does not logically entail sacrifice of excess populations; see 216), it is nonetheless the case that the depoliticized neoliberal subject, buffeted endlessly by economic forces, is deprived of any of the political agency or dignity associated with *bios*.

Agamben pushes the collapse of the *zōē/bios* distinction much further back than Brown, Foucault, or even Arendt. Arendt presents classical Athens as the exemplary moment when the distinction clearly held and presents a narrative where philosophers and theologians, unable to bear the rigors of authentic political action, begin to replace the *vita activa* (*bios*) with the *vita contemplativa*—setting in train the complex sequence of events that will culminate in the modern notion of the "social" and the triumph of the *animal laborans* (*zōē*). By contrast, Agamben argues that the seeds of the distinction's collapse are already present in the Greek political form itself, because political sovereignty has always already been at work collapsing the *zōē/bios* distinction by reducing members of the human political community to the status of victimizable "bare life."

In many ways Agamben's narrative supplements that of Arendt, giving more attention to the Roman household and its influence on the prototo-talitarianism of the Imperial era in both *Homo Sacer* and *State of Exception*.[28] In other ways, however, Agamben reverses Arendt, insofar as his close analysis of book 1 of the *Politics* in *The Use of Bodies* represents the figure of the slave—and not, as in both Arendt and Brown, the master—as the most promising model for a new vision of human life.[29] This reversal reflects the fact that rather than following Arendt and Brown in reasserting *bios* over and against the ravages of an out-of-control *zōē*, the political over the economic, Agamben is aiming at something he calls "form-of-life," which would not so much restore the political-economic dyad to its classical form as side-step it altogether. In other words, instead of attempting to get back to the proper balance between the political and economic that a later tradition has betrayed, Agamben views the distinction itself as the root of the later developments and claims that the only way to escape those destructive effects is to escape or surpass the dyad itself.

Yet the inertia of Arendt's axiom continues to make itself felt in Agamben's project. Alongside this radical proposal to rework all the most fundamental concepts of the Western intellectual tradition, there is a sense that returning to something like the balance represented in the Greek *polis* may represent the "least bad" practical option. In these moments Agamben echoes Arendt's one-sided denigration of the economic realm. In the conclusion of *The Sacrament of Language*, for instance, Agamben bemoans the collapse of the political into the economic (and the concomitant effects on the political action par excellence for Arendt, namely speech): "In a moment when all the European languages seem condemned to swear in vain and when politics can only assume the form of an *oikonomia*, that is, of a governance of empty speech over bare life, it is once more from philosophy that there can come, in the sober awareness of the extreme situation at which the living human being that has language has arrived in its history, the indication of a line of resistance and of change."[30] Though Agamben does not call for a return to the political proper, it is clear that the contemporary order's descent into sheer *oikonomia* (or economy) and empty political speech is a sign of just how bad things have gotten—a diagnosis that Brown would surely share.

Agamben's first extended engagement with the concept of *oikonomia* appears in *The Kingdom and the Glory*, where he declares his intention to "inquire into the paths by which and the reasons why power in the West has assumed the form of an *oikonomia*, that is, a government of human beings."[31] At the time this massive work first appeared—as the unexpected second part to the second volume of the *Homo Sacer* series—this turn toward *oikonomia* seemed to depart from his more recent work on sovereignty and "bare life." Indeed, to the naive reader it might even appear that the paradigm of "economic theology" that he introduces alongside "political theology" is intended to be a positive alternative to Schmitt (1). This impression is reinforced when Agamben restages the debate between Schmitt and the theologian Erik Peterson and argues that for all his harsh criticism of Schmitt, Peterson shares with him the same "conscious repression" of the economic element in the theological texts he is citing (14). Only once we restore the economic to its central role, Agamben claims, can we "identify what is really at stake in the debate between the two friends/enemies about political theology" (14).

The next four chapters of *The Kingdom and the Glory* unfold a complex genealogy of the concept of *oikonomia*, beginning from early Greek thought, moving through the New Testament and patristic authors, and ultimately culminating in the articulation of the doctrine of Divine Providence that, Agamben suggests, serves as the model for the contemporary political-economic order. When he lays out a series of theses on the "providential paradigm" (140–41), several of the features adduced appear to be positive from a modern perspective, such as the necessity of "the division of powers" and the claim that providential governance "is not a despotic power that does violence to the freedom of creatures" but instead "presupposes the freedom of those who are governed" (141). We seem, therefore, to be breaking with the terms of Arendt's axiom, wherein the economic is the realm of necessity and emphatically not the realm of freedom.

Lurking in the background throughout this analysis is another question that Agamben also introduces in his preface: "Why does power need glory? If it is essentially force and capacity for action and government, why does it assume the rigid, cumbersome, and 'glorious' form of ceremonies, acclama-

tions, and protocols? What is the relationship between economy and Glory?"
(xii). The issue of glory initially seems to be simply juxtaposed to the theme
of economy, with no necessary connection between the two, and the first half
of the book barely mentions the theme of glory. Not until the sixth chapter,
"Angelology and Bureaucracy," do the two themes appear together, united
in the theological figure of the angels, who both execute God's providential plan on earth and eternally praise God in heaven. The two functions are
so closely intertwined, in fact, that Agamben can claim that the "caesura"
between praise and governance "cuts through each angel, which is divided
between the two poles that are constitutive of the angelic function" (151).

Agamben's goal in this chapter, however, is to pry the two roles apart.
His first step is to observe that there is a key difference between Christian
and modern notions of economic governance: "the theological economy is
essentially finite. The Christian paradigm of government, like the vision of
history that supports it, lasts from the creation until the end of the world. . . .
[Modernity] abolishes eschatology and infinitely prolongs the history and
government of the world" (163; translation altered). Yet this contrast is
not so clear-cut: "The principle according to which the government of the
world will cease with the Last Judgment has only one important exception
in Christian theology. It is the case of hell" (163). If heaven is filled with
angels who, retired from their administrative functions, have nothing to do
but praise God, hell is the abode of their fallen comrades, the demons, who
can never consciously praise God and yet "will carry out their judicial function as executors of the infernal punishments for all eternity." This means
that "hell is that place in which the divine government of the world survives
for all eternity, even if only in a penitentiary form," and "the demons . . .
will be the indefectible ministers and eternal executioners of divine justice"
(164). This series of observations culminates in a rare joke: "this means that,
from the perspective of Christian theology, the idea of eternal government
(which is the paradigm of modern politics) is truly infernal" (164). And with
that, Agamben definitively turns away from the paradigm of economy as
completely unredeemable, devoting the remainder of his text to an analysis
of glory.

This convoluted argument amounts to what Agamben might call a "forcing." It is internally self-contradictory insofar as the Christian paradigm is

presented as including both a finite and an eternal economy. And it is far from clear why the association between economy and hell in Christian theology is sufficient reason to dismiss the paradigm of economy altogether. After all, Christian theology associates economy equally, if not more so, with salvation and even (as Agamben himself shows in *The Kingdom and the Glory*) with God's own trinitarian life. In any event, Agamben has given us no grounds to simply accept Christian moral valuations in this regard. His case for the ultimate separability of economy and glory is also shaky, because the eternal coexistence of heaven and hell would seem to support exactly the opposite conclusion, namely that they are inseparable. And finally, there is a strange irony in the fact that Agamben, after starting his investigation with the claim that Schmitt and Peterson went wrong by turning away from the concept of economy, should engage in a "conscious repression" of his own by banishing economy to eternal hellfire.

Thus a study that seemed set to overturn Arendt's axiom reasserts it in the most hyperbolic possible way. And once we see the connection with Arendt, Agamben's enigmatic meditations on "inoperativity" appear to be a variation on the theme that the fullest potential of humanity is only to be found beyond the necessity of servile labor. Meanwhile, the relationship between the two paradigms of political theology and economic theology is nowhere clarified. The sharp turn away from economy and toward glory, a theme that Agamben associates with sovereignty despite the fact that he reaches it by way of economic governance, would seem to indicate that the two are somehow separable. Yet not only glory but the political theological theme par excellence, the sovereign exception, can appear as an economic theme, since *oikonomia* takes on the implication of "exception" in the context of Christian pastoral care (49–50). One could infer from this that the realm of economy is where we can find Benjamin's exception that has become the norm, but Agamben does not make this connection explicit in this context. Instead, the implication seems to be that, as in Arendt and Brown's narratives, the economy is illegitimately encroaching on the territory of the political.

What is strange about Agamben's reassertion of Arendt's axiom is that his genealogical narrative undermines many of the normative claims that gave the axiom its force. I have already highlighted the fact that in the providential paradigm, the economic is identified as the realm of freedom, not of constraint and necessity—a clear reversal in Arendt's terms. More broadly, Arendt describes the economic as the realm of the *animal laborans* caught in the endless cycle of natural reproduction, whereas the political is the ever-shifting terrain of surprise and creativity. By contrast, Agamben identifies the political with the "glorious" tedium of pomp and ceremony, while the principle of *oikonomia* is adaptability itself: "*oikonomia* designates a practice and a non-epistemic knowledge that should be assessed only in the context of the aims that they pursue, even if, in themselves, they may appear to be inconsistent with the good" (19). It is telling in this regard that the first conceptual transfer that Agamben documents out of the "proper" realm of the household concerns precisely the field of rhetoric (19–20), which is to say political speech. Though he claims that "the awareness of the original domestic meaning was never lost," in terms of Agamben's own analysis it would make just as much sense to claim that *oikonomia* represents a general logic that was initially discovered in the domestic sphere but of which the household application is only one case among others. Certainly he provides us with no grounds for maintaining a sharp distinction between the economic and the political, much less for privileging the latter—hence, perhaps, the forced and hasty way he demonizes the economic by means of a joke.

Working independently at around the same time Agamben was completing *The Kingdom and the Glory*, Dotan Leshem developed his own genealogy of the concept of *oikonomia*, which also starts from an Arendtian perspective and aims to supplement Foucault's researches into biopolitics and governmentality.[32] There are several notable differences in Leshem's approach—his focus on the period around the Council of Nicea (325 CE) as opposed to Agamben's preference for the previous era of Christian thought, for instance—but the most decisive is his emphasis on more pastoral texts that reflected how Christian bishops conceived their day-to-day practice in terms of *oikonomia*. In this respect Leshem's work functions much more clearly as a supplement to Foucault's research into late medieval and early modern pastoral practice. Leshem is also more explicit about his debt to Arendt, structuring his investigation around a "human trinity" of the economic, the political, and the philosophical sphere that he derives from *The Human Condition*.

I have argued elsewhere that Agamben's genealogy of *oikonomia* can be read as an indirect critique of neoliberalism,[33] but no such deductive work is required in the case of Leshem, who published his findings under the title *The Origins of Neoliberalism*. As it turns out, however, the book engages only briefly with neoliberalism, and as in Agamben's parallel study, the direct genealogical connections with modernity can be characterized as more suggestive than definitive. The key justification behind the title is the claim that Leshem has uncovered in "the Christianity of Late Antiquity . . . *the* transformative moment" in the process by which economy comes to overpower all other aspects of human life (3; italics in original), a process that has culminated in the pan-economism of the neoliberal order.

Leshem's "human trinity" cannot simply be equated to the dyad of Arendt's axiom, and he concludes by expressing his hope that the philosophical, rather than the political, can take the lead in overcoming the planetary sway of the economic (179–81). Yet the logic and structure of his argument depend on the identification of the economic with a discrete and definable aspect of human experience, and as in the case of Agamben, his own genealogical narrative undercuts such a claim. Most notably, he agrees with Agamben that the relationship between economy and politics with respect to freedom completely reverses in the Christian dispensation: where in classical Greece "economy begins with necessity," in Christianity, "economy begins with freedom" (78) while "politics is the kingdom of necessity and suppression" (121). And Leshem's description of the flexible—and at times even underhanded (29)—conduct of bishops carrying out their economic function of growing God's kingdom sounds much more like the kind of open-ended, unpredictable action Arendt associates with the political than like anything she would attribute to the humble *animal laborans*. Leshem's investigation could almost be read as a critique of Arendt's axiom, if not for the fact that a version of that axiom provides the basis for his claim to be tracing "the origins of neoliberalism."

Alternative Approaches

In *The Kingdom and the Glory* Agamben laments the paucity of scholarship on the role of *oikonomia* in Christian thought, most of which focuses on individual figures or time periods. Among the works he names is Marie-José Mondzain's *Image, Icon, Economy*, which he counts as a narrowly specialized treatment because it "limits itself to analyzing the implications of this concept for the iconoclastic disputes that took place between the eighth and ninth centuries" in the Byzantine Empire (2).[34] Leshem also treats the book as a specialized study, arguing briefly with specific points in footnotes (185nn3–5).

In reality, though, Mondzain's text displays the same ambition and philosophical rigor as Agamben's and Leshem's but without the blinders of Arendt's axiom. Thus, like Agamben, Mondzain is concerned with the relationship between economy and glory (in the sense of spectacle and image), and like Leshem, she is engaged with the political, economic, and philosophical dimensions of human experience. Yet she comes to the material with no prior commitments about what distinctions do or should hold in either case, nor with any pregiven value judgments about the "proper" place of the economic. A scholar and translator of the iconophile Patriarch of Constantinople Nikephorus, she is concerned to let her materials speak to the contemporary world on their own terms, while eschewing the easy answers proffered by more pious scholars.[35] She can straightforwardly characterize economy as "a philosophical and political concept"[36]—at once disregarding Arendt's axiom and sidestepping Agamben's claim in *The Kingdom and the Glory* that "economy" must be identified not as a concept but as a "signature" (4–5). And from this perspective Mondzain is not surprised or disturbed to find that the concept of *oikonomia* is central in the debate over images, nor does she hesitate to characterize that struggle as one that is at once political (defying the iconoclastic emperor who wishes to hoard the power of images for himself)[37] and philosophical (requiring sophisticated argumentation to achieve the apparent reversal of the biblical prohibition of images).

Recounting fully Mondzain's argument would take us far afield of the present study, but her overall method can serve as a model for the general theory of political theology that I am aiming for. Mondzain shares with political theology the basic refusal of the religious-political dyad, as shown equally in her dismissal of recent edifying studies of the icon's religious role and in her bold assertion of the contemporary relevance of the theological problem she is studying.[38] She moves fluidly among the political, the economic, and the philosophical, without presupposing any normative boundaries between them and without risking reductionism by putting forward any one factor as fundamental. This means that she is as attentive as Foucault to the many and varied weapons that find their way into a power struggle, but at the same time, she also anticipates what I am calling a general political theology by taking seriously the normative claims that motivate the opponents.

At the same time, though, Mondzain does not offer much concrete guidance for an investigation of the neoliberal order. Although Agamben and Leshem may have paid her work insufficient attention, they were not wrong to see in it primarily a specialist work focused on a distant historical period with only a tenuous claim to contemporary relevance. More immediately helpful are a series of treatments of the neoliberal order from a theological perspective—namely, Mark C. Taylor's *Confidence Games*, Philip Goodchild's *Theology of Money*, Joshua Ramey's *Politics of Divination*, and Eric Santner's *The Weight of All Flesh*—each of which in its own way shares in Mondzain's disregard for the arbitrary boundaries that are supposed to separate the political, religious, economic, and philosophical realms. As such, although only Santner's study explicitly claims the mantle of political theology, each is able to achieve the kind of stunning defamiliarization of our present moment that has always been political theology's stock in trade.

Taylor's work is in many ways the most path-breaking. Predating even Harvey's *Brief History of Neoliberalism*, which arguably inaugurated the shift in focus from neoconservatism to neoliberalism on the academic left, Taylor provides not only an account of neoliberalism but a complete theory of culture that brings together the theological, the economic, and the aesthetic realms into a coherent whole. He is unique among commentators in humanities disciplines in being relatively optimistic, even enthusiastic, about the neoliberal order. This is doubtless due in part to his experience in founding an educational start-up called the Global Education Network, which gave him the opportunity to act as a "participant-observer" at the intersection of computer technology and high finance[39]—a much more positive encounter with the neoliberal order than most academics, bogged down in assessment rubrics and scholarly impact evaluations, can boast.

More fundamentally, though, his apparent optimism stems from the fact that Taylor does not seek to impose a normative vision on contemporary reality, an effort that he associates with the failed command economies of the Eastern Bloc,[40] but instead starts from the recognition that "we are entering a new territory and need new maps."[41] In this regard he believes that neoliberal economists and financiers alike have been just as guilty as the Soviets of clinging to an outdated model—namely, the Efficient Markets Hypothesis, which wrongly presupposes that markets have a tendency to return to equilibrium. Hence Taylor attempts to be more neoliberal than the neoliberals themselves, developing a new conceptual model, drawn from complex systems theory, that can better respond to the new challenges presented by an increasingly networked world. From a certain perspective, then, Taylor is taking the bold step of putting himself forward as a theologian of neoliberalism, or perhaps its prophet, warning the entrepreneurs and financiers of the world to flee the coming crisis by discarding the old wineskins of their outdated economic models in favor of a new theory of culture that truly answers to the demands of the present.

Goodchild is a theologian of the neoliberal order in a different sense. Rather than attempt to devise a normative theology *for* neoliberalism, Goodchild wishes to discern the theology that is already implicit in the practice of capitalism itself. His investigation is perhaps the most explicit example of the broader approach to "theology" that I am associating with a general political theology. Goodchild is not saying that contemporary capitalist practice is metaphorically "like" theology, nor is he claiming (with Taylor, Agamben, and Leshem) that economic theory has "roots" in theology. He is saying that capitalism directly implies its *own* theology, centered on money as the Tillichian "ultimate concern." In a world where money is effectively God, Goodchild asks, what theology is implied? While he draws extensively on economic theory, Goodchild is much more concerned with the history and practice of finance. Particularly illuminating is his presentation of setting a price as an "act of faith," based not on objective facts but on "hopes and expectations, uncertainties and strategies." This means that "each act of pricing is a guess, an estimate or approximation. Since there is nothing to which it approximates, then pricing is always an act of faith. It is inherently theological."[42] From that perspective, financial accounting is less an objective science than an ascetic discipline, a series of rituals that a firm must carry out to show that it is a faithful steward of its resources.[43]

Ramey also associates neoliberal practice with the realm of ritual, and, uniquely among theologically informed critics of neoliberalism, it is not

Christian ritual that he has in mind. Instead, he claims that "neoliberal market fundamentalism—the view that markets alone can resolve the problem of how to construct social life in the face of unforeseeable contingencies—is a perverse and disavowed colonization of archaic divination rites, the rituals through which human cultures, on the basis of chance, have perennially sought for more-than-human knowledge."[44] Although he does not propose a full-blown theory of religion, Ramey identifies "tacit or explicit evaluations of the *mysterium tremendum et fascinans* that the unknown and unforeseeable represent" as calling forth different forms of piety in different historical periods. The problem is not that neoliberalism is a form of divination or piety toward the contingent—Ramey is not a secularist deploying "primitive religion" polemically to delegitimate neoliberalism—but that it does not recognize itself as such, meaning that it "has managed to render its own politics of divination incontestable."[45]

In the previous chapter, I defined the root of political theology as the need to respond to the deadlock represented by the problem of evil and the problem of legitimacy. Ramey's "archaic and perennial problem of how to meaningfully interpret the deliverances of chance" could be interpreted as another articulation of that same deadlock.[46] What is the problem of evil and suffering but the problem of how to cope with what we cannot, by definition, predict or control? And what presents a greater challenge to a political order than its failure to anticipate or compensate for an unforeseen disaster? In this sense Ramey's project, though it is not explicitly situated in terms of political theology,[47] is broadly homologous to my own. He also provides resources for the present chapter's concern to break down the political-economic binary by highlighting the deeply *political* character of market competition, as when he points out that "the conversion of all sociality into market-like processes has introduced dispute and judgment everywhere,"[48] making the economic realm the center of the kind of agonistic competition that Arendt associates with the political. And in his reading of Vico's account of the place of divination in the class struggles that defined primitive Roman society,[49] he makes it clear that what is at stake in the competition over the right to divination is prestige and honor—in a word, glory.

We are thus back where Agamben began: the connection between economy and glory. It is this connection that is not so much interrogated as presupposed in one of the only existing studies to explicitly take up political theology as a primary lens for understanding the neoliberal predicament, namely, Eric Santner's *The Weight of All Flesh*. In his previous book, *The Royal Remains*, Santner had advanced a synthesis of psychoanalysis and political theology in order to construct a narrative of the transition to modernity wherein the "stuff" of the king's sovereign body was dispersed into the bodies of the people.[50] Here he argues that the "spectral materiality" of sovereignty was subsequently displaced into the surplus value congealed in the commodity. This leads Santner to risk a bold reading of Marx's theory of commodity fetishism as a theory of glory, a reading that he connects with Weber's well-known narrative of the "spirit" of capitalism that demands that we "never cease to economize, and all *for the greater glory of God.*" In other words, "the Protestant Ethic effectively transforms work itself into a sort of obsessive-compulsive *doxology*, the liturgical praise or glorification of God," a ritual observance that contemporary capitalism unwittingly continues.[51]

All four of these studies provide models for the project of a political theology of neoliberalism. All four insist on the theological character of the neoliberal order, from both a genealogical and a synchronic perspective. They also display the kind of disciplinary promiscuity that marks political theology, even in its narrowly Schmittian form. Ramey and Santner, in particular, implicitly overcome Arendt's axiom when they show how political features (competition and struggle, glory and ceremonial) come to define the supposedly purely economic realm of neoliberalism. Yet both are still working within the terms of a qualitative distinction between the political and the economic. For Ramey, the political aspects represent the unintentional blowback of neoliberalism's attempt to extinguish the political, while for Santner, the political/glorious side of neoliberalism represents a kind of uncanny leftover of the more properly political phenomenon of pre-Revolutionary monarchical sovereignty. In both cases we are once again dealing with the ostensibly surprising revelation that what "should" be a solely economic phenomenon also displays political features.

Beyond Arendt's Axiom

My question at this point is why, even when it does not appear as a betrayal or fall from grace, this intermingling of the political and the economic should come as a surprise. Literally every single genealogical narrative we have investigated so far—including, above all, those that are most invested in Arendt's axiom—has shown that the Athenian model lionized by Arendt is the exception, not the norm. Virtually every feature of human experience that is supposed to be properly political in Arendtian terms has appeared in the economic realm in later eras. What possible basis is there for clinging to the Arendtian distinction as a norm or even as a foil?

One might be tempted to reply that neoliberalism presents itself as the economic overcoming of politics. And it is true that neoliberalism puts forward such a face, which is itself an interesting fact that I will attempt to account for in the next chapter. Yet it does not take much critical acumen to see through the vulgar libertarianism with which neoliberal ideologues seek to veil a regime in which state action is absolutely pervasive. To believe that a violation of simplistic libertarianism represents a contradiction or an unintended consequence is ultimately an all-too-sophisticated way of falling for neoliberalism's ideological framing by taking it more seriously than it deserves or even intends to be taken.

A political theological approach does incorporate the normative claims that underwrite a given paradigm, but that means putting aside opportunistic sales pitches aimed at a mass audience and paying closer attention to what the most intellectually rigorous proponents of that paradigm say to each other. We have already discussed one good example of the latter: Milton Friedman's "Neo-Liberalism and Its Prospects." In that speech Friedman describes neoliberalism as a political agenda to install a certain economic order that reflects a set of normative principles about how human society is and ought to be structured. If we take Friedman at his word that this is the kind of thing neoliberalism is or at least wants to be, then Arendt's axiom would provide us with strong grounds to lament neoliberalism's perversion of the true meaning of politics and perhaps even to inscribe neoliberalism into a longer narrative of decline and betrayal. Yet that axiom would provide us with very little analytic purchase on neoliberalism in its historical specificity, much less any guidance for how to transform or overcome it.

This is not to say that concepts of the political and the economic have no meaning or value. Without those categories it would be very difficult to talk about neoliberalism at all. They are closely intertwined and lack a definitive boundary, but that does not mean that distinctions between them cannot be analytically helpful. Nor should my argument be taken to mean that the genealogical study of the concept of *oikonomia* is a blind alley. Agamben, Leshem, and Mondzain have all contributed substantially to our knowledge of economic phenomena, opening up a productive path of research that other scholars continue to build on.

What I am suggesting is that their adherence to Arendt's axiom has rendered Agamben's and Leshem's accounts insufficiently genealogical. And here I have in mind Nietzsche's methodological credo from *The Genealogy of Morals*, where he declares that "the cause of the origin of a thing and its eventual utility, its actual employment and place in a system of purposes, lie worlds apart; whatever exists, having somehow come into being, is again and again reinterpreted to new ends, taken over, transformed, and redirected by some power superior to it." This implies that "the entire history of a 'thing,' an organ, a custom can in this way be a continuous sign-chain of ever new interpretations and adaptations whose causes do not even have to be related to one another but, on the contrary, in some cases succeed and alternate with one another in a purely chance fashion."[52]

For a truly *genealogical* genealogy of economy, the kinds of displacements and reversals we have seen would represent neither a surprise nor a betrayal but a baseline expectation. Granting that the Greeks have bequeathed to the Western tradition a certain tension between the political and the economic, a genealogical investigation would not lament but positively expect that the relationship between the two would be continually reconfigured—sometimes to the point of near-unrecognizability—in the ongoing power struggle that is history. And that would mean recognizing that "the political" and "the economic" are not and cannot be static unities. Instead, the distinction itself can be viewed as an apparatus for distributing power and authority by means of the distribution of other important binaries: freedom vs. necessity, artifice vs. nature, deliberation vs. spontaneity, equality vs. hierarchy, or contestation vs. harmony.

In the original Aristotelian model, the binaries as listed here are all made to reflect the overarching binary of political vs. economic so that, for instance, the organization of the household is what happens spontaneously and naturally while the city requires a higher degree of deliberate construction.

Where the political for Aristotle is the place for equality and contestation, the household, by contrast, displays a harmonious hierarchical order. None of these distinctions is absolute or exclusive—for instance, the city is also "natural" in the sense of being the goal toward which human associations do or should tend—but they underwrite a harmonious social order in which every important aspect of human experience is represented and the highest human aspirations find space and support.

Yet even on its own terms, Aristotle's idyllic *polis* is menaced from within by a binary that emerges from the household itself: the distinction between legitimate household management (*oikonomia*) and out-of-control acquisition by means of money and market exchange (*chrēmatistikē*, which Joe Sachs translates as "provisioning"). Whereas the former is bounded by the goal of "living well," the latter is completely "unlimited" and hence unnatural.[53] Though it cannot be eliminated entirely, the drive for acquisition must not be allowed free rein, lest it completely displace the pursuit of "living well."

It was on the basis of this distinction that one of the greatest theorists of the Fordist order, Karl Polanyi, declared Aristotle's *Politics* "certainly still the best analysis of the subject we possess" because it acknowledges the dangers associated with markets, and particularly with money, but nevertheless recognizes that "as long as markets and money were mere accessories to an otherwise self-sufficient household, the principle of production for use could operate."[54] In other words, Polanyi views Aristotle as an early exponent of his own project of preserving what he calls "society" from the corrosive effects of market forces. Much the same could be said of Arendt, for whom Aristotle represents a critic of mass consumer society *avant la lettre*.

While one could accuse Arendt or Polanyi of misreading Aristotle on a detailed level, there is nonetheless something appropriate about their gesture. A genealogical perspective invites us to recognize that just as they attempt to borrow Aristotle's cultural authority to advance their political agendas, so also was Aristotle himself intervening politically in a cultural context where increased reliance on foreign trade and greater emphasis on monetary wealth threatened to undermine traditional social hierarchies and institutions. Aristotle's text, in other words, does not so much reflect or discover a norm as attempt to *impose* one on a changing world. And at least in his distinction between legitimate household management and out-of-control acquisition, he was more successful than he ever could have imagined, as his authority backed up a millennium and more of usury bans and trade restrictions in the Christian and Islamic worlds alike. If that authority no longer functions as an effective weapon in the neoliberal order, it is because the advocates of out-of-control acquisition have recruited the forces of family and morality to their side. It is to that disturbing development that we now turn.

CHAPTER 3

NEOLIBERALISM'S DEMONS

Polanyi famously characterized the interplay between market forces and society as a "double movement": when market relations threaten to undermine the basic foundations of social reproduction, society (most often represented by state institutions) intervenes to prevent or at least delay the trend set in motion by the market. Compared with Aristotle's distribution of categories between the political and economic realms, Polanyi's account is itself a "great transformation" on the conceptual level. Where Aristotle distinguished state and household and placed both legitimate economic management and unrestrained accumulation in the latter, Polanyi's "society" combines the household and the state, leaving only out-of-control acquisition in the purely economic realm. And in this schema, society represents the spontaneous and natural, while the economic force of the market is what is constructed and deliberate.

This latter point may appear initially contradictory, since the "double movement" portrays the state primarily as reactive to market forces. As Polanyi points out, however, markets do not simply spring up naturally but have historically been created and cultivated by state actors—something that is above all true of the global market of the nineteenth century. At the same time, by creating the conditions for a worldwide, self-regulating market, governments were unleashing forces that they would later be forced to contain. Polanyi neatly captures this paradox: "While laissez-faire economy was the product of deliberate State action, subsequent restrictions on laissez-faire started in a spontaneous way. Laissez-faire was planned; planning was not."[1]

Writing in 1944, Polanyi's account of the relation between society and the market reflected the deep presuppositions that would shape the emerging postwar order known as Fordism. And as Melinda Cooper points out, Polanyi's analysis has proven quite durable in the post-Fordist era, as his "thesis of the 'double movement' is pervasive and well-nigh uncontested in contemporary left-wing formulations of anticapitalist critique."[2] One of Cooper's primary ambitions in her bold reexamination of the interplay between neoliberalism and social conservatism in the last forty years of American politics is to displace Polanyi's theory. At the heart of her critique is the observation that "Polanyi imagines the countermovement [of society against market corrosion] as external to the dynamics of capitalism and yet historically inevitable and indeed necessitated by the free market itself" so that within his framework "resistance can only be imagined as conservative" (14).

The legacy of Polanyi should already be familiar to us in the many analyses of neoliberalism that see the state, nationalism, and other similar forces as extrinsic "leftovers" that precede or exceed neoliberal logic. Normally such interpretations first point out the supposed irony or hypocrisy that neoliberalism comes to require these exogenous elements for its functioning while claiming that those same "leftover" institutions can be sites of resistance. Hence, for instance, one often hears that the left needs to restore confidence in state power over against the market, that socialism can only be viable if a given country isolates itself from the forces of the global market, or in Wendy Brown's more abstract terms, that the left must reclaim the political to combat the hegemony of the economic.

The goal of the previous chapter was to demonstrate that critiques of neoliberalism based on binaries between the political and the economic are ultimately self-undermining. Cooper's argument shows that the same can be said for the other institutions that make up Polanyi's "society": above all the family, but also race and religion. Her guiding assumption is that "what Polanyi calls the 'double movement' would be better understood as fully internal to the dynamic of capital" (15). While capitalism is undoubtedly corrosive of traditional institutions, Cooper asks rhetorically, "is it not also compelled to reassert the reproductive institutions of race, family, and nation as a way of ensuring the unequal distribution of wealth and income across time? Isn't it compelled, in the last instance, to reinstate the family as the elementary legal form of private wealth accumulation?" (18). And we can adapt this notion to specific phases of capitalism: neoliberalism does not simply destroy some preexisting entity known as "the family," but creates *its own* version of the family, one that fits its political-economic agenda, just as Fordism created the white suburban nuclear family that underwrote its political-economic goals.

Neoliberalism achieves this transformation of the family not by deploying economic as opposed to political tools, nor by setting unfettered Aristotelian acquisition over against "natural" household management. Rather, neoliberalism carries out its own "great transformation" by reconfiguring the relationship between the political and the economic and reimagining the household precisely as a site of indefinite accumulation. As Cooper points out, the explosion of inherited wealth, in the wake of an era in which its importance had declined precipitously, was not an accidental or unforeseen result of neoliberal policy but an explicit attempt to create greater incentives for capital accumulation. Nor indeed were cuts to welfare programs motivated solely or even primarily by a desire for an abstractly "smaller" and less costly government. Rather, neoliberals recognized that "the dismantling of welfare represents the most effective means of restoring the private bonds of familial obligation" (60), as those deprived of an impersonal public safety net will be forced to rely on a familial private safety net. Hence, in this political moment, both neoliberals and neoconservatives can "seize upon the necessity of family responsibility as the ideal source of economic security and an effective counterforce to the demoralizing powers of the welfare state" (73).

Cooper's revisionist history also highlights a factor that rarely receives extended attention in accounts of neoliberalism: race. The Fordist nuclear family that the state subsidized both directly (through welfare provisions) and indirectly (through subsidies encouraging homeownership) was figured explicitly as white, and in Cooper's telling, the definitive transition from Fordism to neoliberalism can be traced to the reaction against a demand to extend the guarantee of the "family wage" for a male breadwinner to black families.[3] That the legacy of slavery should prove decisive will come as no surprise to any student of American history. Nor should readers of Aristotle be taken aback, since in his account, home economics are deeply entwined with the question of slavery. Indeed, the master-slave relationship is discussed earlier and at greater length than the other relationships (marriage, parenting) that appear much more central to the life of the household from a modern perspective. In these same passages, Aristotle engages in speculations that resonate with modern conceptions of racial slavery, above all when he claims that "nature intends to make the bodies of free people and slaves differ, one sort strong for necessary service, the other upright and useless for labors of that kind, but useful for a political life."[4] In Aristotle's view, nature does not manage to achieve this goal in practice, but centuries later, white slave masters claimed to find in the black body an inherent enslavability. And even when blacks were formally emancipated, it remained (and arguably still remains) an open question whether black men would be allowed to be heads of households alongside whites or would instead be consigned to servile labor.

And here arises another question that seldom comes to the fore in accounts of neoliberalism: that of gender, in the form of the ideal that a wife's place should be in the home. From this perspective it makes sense that the welfare program that came in for the greatest criticism, despite making up a trivial portion of the federal budget, was Aid to Families with Dependent Children (AFDC). Toward the end of the 1970s, a series of legal challenges resulted in "revised AFDC rules [that] allowed divorced or never-married women and their children to live independently of a man while receiving a state-guaranteed income free of moral conditions."[5] The specter of state-sponsored woman-headed households and the demand for blacks to enjoy the privileges of the Fordist family wage converged in the figure of the black "welfare queen," who enjoys a life of luxury at the hardworking taxpayer's expense. Within the ideological narrative, the welfare queen does not simply victimize the broader community through her parasitism, but she comes to embody the moral crisis that was reflected in the inflation crisis of the late 1970s. In short, the welfare queen exercises a near-demonic power over American society, far out of proportion to what the poverty of actual welfare recipients would lead us to expect.

My goal in this chapter is to demonstrate that it is no accident that a demonized figure like the welfare queen proved so instrumental in America's transition to neoliberalism. I have previously spoken of the ways that Brown and Agamben demonize neoliberalism, and in the present chapter I am going to do the reverse: to show how neoliberalism demonizes *us*. In this argument I will push my general theory of political theology to the limit by inverting the dominant approach: whereas most political theological accounts focus on the parallel between God and his earthly counterpart, I will argue that it is the parallel between God's demonic foes and the social order's subjugated populations that is most decisive for our understanding of neoliberalism.

Making this argument will also require a different approach to genealogy. I will be attending to the *locus classicus* of the transition from medieval Christianity to modernity, but I will do so by emphasizing the birth of capitalism in place of the usual one-sided focus on the birth of the modern state. And where most genealogical narratives in political theology attempt to unmask the unconscious, forgotten, or repressed theological origins of political institutions, I will primarily (though not exclusively) treat neoliberalism as a *self-conscious* attempt to return to the founding moment of global capitalism—a moment that had itself witnessed the instrumentalization of religion to discipline and scapegoat entire populations, above all through the rhetoric of demonization. Having established this connection, I will briefly review representative sources in an attempt to specify more exactly how demonization functions in Christian theology before turning to the many and varied ways that neoliberalism demonizes individuals and entire populations, with an emphasis on the distinctions of race and nation that neoliberalism supposedly renders obsolete. This political-theological account of neoliberalism will then serve as the basis for my final chapter, which will investigate the reactionary populist wave represented by the Brexit vote and the Trump presidency and the question of whether it makes sense to view these phenomena as betokening the "end" of neoliberalism.

Returning to the "Satanic Mill"

Even if one accepts Cooper's critique, Polanyi does have a great deal to offer critics of the neoliberal age. Indeed, for a reader versed in neoliberalism, the narrative of *The Great Transformation* provokes a shock of recognition—or, better, an uncanny sense of retrospective *déjà vu*. In Polanyi's account, as I have noted, the establishment of the supposedly autonomous, self-regulating market was not something that came about spontaneously but through concerted political action. One of the most decisive moments in the British context was the abolition of a set of laws that guaranteed a basic level of subsistence to all the common people, laws that were widely viewed as self-undermining and destructive in their effects.[6] The parallel with the destruction of the welfare state, which was similarly blamed for economic stagnation, is clear. Other major points in his narrative invite comparisons to the last several decades of political-economic history as well: his account of how governments became obsessed with fiscal solvency and monetary stability to the near exclusion of all other concerns, for instance, or of how powerful international financial institutions took on a de facto governance role that allowed them to dictate terms to all but the most powerful states.

More telling for my purposes, however, are Polanyi's repeated references to colonialism and the slave trade. Given his focus on the "One-Hundred Years Peace" on the European continent, these remarks could seem like incidental asides, but taken together, they amount to an insistent subtheme that highlights the violence at the heart of the free market. The most extended discussion comes in a section where he argues, against the idealized vision of free-market dogmatists, that "the Inferno of early capitalism" was in fact as bad as contemporary accounts had made it out to be. Against the contention that the amazing economic growth of the era healed all wounds, he contends that the real damage was "a social calamity" that cannot "be measured by income figures or population statistics."[7]

Polanyi admits that there are not many points of comparison because of the infrequency of "cataclysmic events like the Industrial Revolution—an economic earthquake which transformed within less than half a century vast masses of the inhabitants of the English countryside from settled folk into shiftless migrants." The imposition of such a radical social change by one class upon another within the same country is very rare indeed, but Polanyi claims that "such destructive landslides . . . are a common occurrence in the sphere of culture contact between peoples of various races. Intrinsically, the conditions are the same. The difference is mainly that a social class forms part of a society inhabiting the same geographical area, while culture contact occurs usually between societies settled in different geographical regions."[8] In those cases, as in the Industrial Revolution, the primary damage is not "economic exploitation, as often assumed, but the disintegration of the cultural

environment of the victim," or in other words "the lethal injury to the institutions in which his social existence is embodied," which leads to "a loss of
self-respect and standards." And in the paragraph that follows, he gives the
concrete example of the "condition of some native tribes in modern [mean-
ing colonial] Africa," which is every bit as degraded as "that of the English
laboring classes during the early years of the nineteenth century."[9] Despite
this obvious parallel, however, "the social historian fails to take the hint. He
still refuses to see that the elemental force of culture contact, which is now
revolutionizing the colonial world, is the same which, a century ago, created
the dismal scenes of early capitalism."[10] In other words, the benighted social
historian fails to see that the Industrial Revolution amounted to a kind of
preemptive self-colonization.

A similar parallel has been observed by a contemporary historian of capitalism, Silvia Federici. While teaching in Nigeria in the mid-1980s, Federici
witnessed the country's "adoption of a Structural Adjustment Program, the
World Bank's universal recipe for economic recovery across the planet." The
process, as she describes it, echoes in many ways Polanyi's narrative: "The
declared purpose of the program was to make Nigeria competitive on the international market. But it was soon apparent that this involved a new round
of primitive accumulation, and a rationalization of social reproduction aimed
at destroying the last vestiges of communal property and community relations, and thereby impose more intense forms of labor exploitation." In other
respects, however, Federici's account is much different. First, with Cooper
she emphasizes the fact that market relations do not one-sidedly destroy
existing social relationships but seek to shape "the reproduction of the workforce" and "regulate procreation rates," which in the Nigerian context took
the form of an effort to "reduce the size of a population that was deemed
too demanding and indisciplined from the viewpoint of its prospected inser-
tion in the global economy." Second, and again anticipating Cooper, Federici
is more attentive to the role of ideological discourse in this effort, a discourse that—in stark contrast to the brutal amorality Polanyi associates with
capitalist apologetics—takes on a distinctively moralizing tone: "Along with
these policies, aptly named the 'War Against Indiscipline,' I also witnessed
the fueling of a misogynous campaign denouncing women's vanity and excessive demands, and the development of a heated debate similar, in many

respects, to the 17th-century *querelles des femmes*, touching on every aspect of the reproduction of labor-power: the family (polygamous vs. monogamous, nuclear vs. extended), child-raising, women's work, male and female identity and relations."[11] The imposition of neoliberal structural adjustment, then, just like the original imposition of capitalism in Western Europe, is for Federici not an economic *as opposed to* social process, nor is it a process that seeks only to destroy society and get it out of the way. Rather, it is an equally economic and social process that actively seeks to reshape society into a form that can support and reproduce capitalist relations, using coercive as well as discursive forces (such as moral exhortation or scapegoating).

Federici also views the parallel between colonization and the initial imposition of capitalism as much closer than Polanyi seems to envision. Whereas Polanyi sees colonization as a later development, Federici sees the two processes as inextricably intertwined from the very beginning in a single process of domination and exploitation. In particular, she highlights the ways that ideological weapons moved promiscuously between the colonies and the metropole, which serve to demonstrate that "capitalism, as a social-economic system, is necessarily committed to racism and sexism." This is because "capitalism must *justify* and *mystify* the contradictions built into its social relations—the promise of freedom vs. the reality of widespread coercion, and the promise of prosperity vs. the reality of widespread penury—by denigrating the 'nature' of those it exploits: women, colonial subjects, the descendants of African slaves, the immigrants displaced by globalization."[12] I emphasize the words *justify* and *mystify* to suggest that Federici could serve as another model for my general theory of political theology, with its concern for discourses of legitimacy and theodicy. But Federici's work is connected with political theology in a narrower sense as well, given that she focuses on the role of religious rhetoric and institutions in the transition to capitalism, particularly in the phenomenon of witch hunts. Far from an unfortunate holdover of medieval superstition, she views the witch hunts as a systematic campaign of terror meant to destroy women's control over the reproductive process. The techniques of this crusade evolved over time through cross-fertilization between antiwitch campaigns in the colonies and the metropole and were eventually adapted to the task of creating and reproducing racial divisions within the global proletariat.[13]

This perspective on the witch hunts highlights another difference between Federici and Polanyi: the place of the demonic. Admittedly, with
Polanyi we are dealing with a pattern of metaphors rather than a sustained
argument, but the pattern is telling. I quoted above his invocation of "the
Inferno of early capitalism," and within that metaphorical context, it is clear
who the demonic torturers are: the free market ideologues, who seek to con-
fine the people in a "Satanic mill" where they will be subject to the brutally
efficient discipline of hunger. On a moral level these attacks are of course
justified, but they are misleading historically because within mainstream discourse the demons were precisely those most victimized by the system. And
as the example of the witch hunt shows, the demonization went beyond un-
kind rhetoric, leading directly to practices of coercion, torture, and execution.
Nor is it a matter of mere historical curiosity, because, Federici points out,
the same things continue to happen in the countries most afflicted by neoliberal structural adjustment:

> The witch hunts that are presently taking place in Africa or Latin America
> are rarely reported in Europe and the United States, in the same way as the
> witch hunts of the 16th and 17th centuries, for a long time, were of little
> interest to historians. Even when they are reported their significance is gen-
> erally missed, so widespread is the belief that such phenomena belong to a
> far-gone era and have nothing to do with "us." . . . If we apply to the pres-
> ent the lessons of the past, we realize that the appearance of witch-hunting
> in so many parts of the world in the 80s and 90s is a clear sign of a process
> of "primitive accumulation," which means that the privatization of land and
> other communal resources, mass impoverishment, plunder, and the sowing of
> divisions in once-cohesive communities are again on the world agenda. . . . In
> some countries, this process still requires the mobilization of witches, spirits,
> and devils. But we should not delude ourselves that this is not our concern.[14]

I would echo Federici's exhortation here, with the proviso that the number of
countries where neoliberalization "still requires the mobilization of witches,
spirits, and devils" may also include the United States.

I have already referred to the "welfare queen," that racialized figure of
sexual license who depletes the public purse with her lavish lifestyle. One
might be tempted to dismiss my evocation of her "demonic" character as a

mere metaphor, but a number of the tropes that accumulated around her bear a striking similarity to what we find in an early modern witch-hunting manual such as the infamous *Malleus Maleficarum* (*Hammer of Witches*, 1468).[15] The same kind of open contradiction is present: the "welfare queen" is defined at once by her poverty (hence her need for welfare payments) and her paradoxical wealth, while the witch is defined as almost all-powerful precisely because of her resentment of her low social standing. On the specifically sexual level, just as the "welfare queen" is supposedly eager to have extra children solely to gain more welfare benefits and yet at the same time constantly obtaining abortions, so too does the witch at once cooperate with demons to father monstrous children and seek to impede childbirth through infanticide or the removal of male genitalia.[16] And where the "welfare queen" has the mysterious ability to cause mass inflation and economic stagnation, the witch possesses the even more awesome power of "depopulating the whole of Christianity."[17]

The Christian legacy of misogyny in our contemporary world should be obvious: the scapegoating of single motherhood, promiscuity, birth control, and abortion are all centered in explicitly religious circles. And there is good warrant for connecting that misogyny to discourses of witchcraft and demonic influences: not only did the rise of neoliberalism correlate with a marked revival of the rhetoric of evil in American politics,[18] but it also witnessed a resurgence of interest in the demonic and in apocalyptic religion more generally. Among the manifestations of this trend was the panic over so-called Satanic Ritual Abuse, a completely fabricated trend that echoed many of the tropes of traditional witch-hunting and for a time garnered the attention of serious researchers and mainstream media outlets. The 1980s and 1990s were also a fertile period for "end times" speculations that attempted to predict the precise timing of the end of the world and identified political opponents with the demonic forces envisioned in biblical prophecy.

One might be tempted to dismiss such phenomena as marginal, but they helped to solidify the sense of urgency that mobilized the religious right in ever-increasing numbers up through George W. Bush's reelection campaign. And as Cooper documents, the religious right was not simply a voting bloc, but became virtually an arm of government as the state moved to outsource a whole range of social services to private charities, with an increasing preference for explicitly "faith-based" providers. In a twist on the Foucauldian narrative of this period, Cooper claims, "What looked like the deinstitution-alization of the disciplinary asylum, then, from another angle could be seen as the *reinstitutionalization of religion*, a process whereby religious charities resumed their once central role in the management of poverty but this time fully integrated into the contractual networks and budgetary calculations of the state."[19] Prison education programs, mental health services, and homeless shelters came to be increasingly dominated by evangelical Christian groups, subjecting the most vulnerable and excluded populations in American soci-ety to religious indoctrination and moral discipline as a condition of basic care: "Evangelical missions practice overt forms of proselytization, holding their clients in an unspoken pact whereby food and shelter are exchanged for evangelism."[20]

In Cooper's telling, the role of the religious right in welfare provision is part of an increasingly seamless alliance between neoliberals and neo-conservatives when it comes to promoting family structures that support capital accumulation. This alliance is not without conflict—for instance, over gay marriage, which neoliberals tend to support and neoconservatives to abhor—but overall it has delivered nearly four decades of remarkably con-sistent bipartisan social policy. What Cooper does not mention is the extent to which the neoconservatives par excellence, the religious right, have con-formed increasingly to neoliberal culture, with most groups lying somewhere along the spectrum between the corporate slickness of the evangelical mega-church and the outright worship of wealth that characterizes the prosperity gospel.[21] And here again we can see a convergence between the margins and the metropole, as recent studies of the Pentecostal wave in the Third World have emphasized the prominent role of the prosperity gospel there.[22] Appar-ently the neoliberal axiom "There Is No Alternative" holds increasingly in the spiritual realm as well, where the greatest aspiration is worldly success.

How to Create a Demon

How can we account for this striking affinity between neoliberalism—a cosmopolitan, materialistic, and often seemingly amoral ideology—and con-servative religion? The parallels between Federici's and Cooper's accounts may tempt us to explain it as a case of history repeating itself: if neoliberalism is an attempt to "reboot" capitalism in the wake of welfare state reforms and the challenge of Real Socialism, then perhaps it stands to reason that it would use the same tools as in the original imposition of capitalism. Yet such an approach would still need to explain the early modern alliance between the tradition-destroying forces of capitalism and precisely the most reactionary and intolerant representatives of traditional religion.

I believe that this conjuncture cannot be explained away as mere coincidence or opportunism. A deeper conceptual link is at work. Taylor, Agamben, and Leshem have all shown the genealogical links that connect modern economic thinking with Christian conceptions of divine providence, and Taylor has demonstrated most forcefully that the Christian legacy is still very much at work in specifically neoliberal accounts of the market. To paraphrase Schmitt, all significant concepts of the modern theory of the market are secularized providential concepts.[23] And that means that they are also *moral* concepts, because the doctrine of divine providence is not solely about the logistics of the divine administration of the world but is concerned above all with vindicating God's justice—in other words, with the problem of evil.[24]

In the mature form that it had reached by the dawn of the modern era, the doctrine of divine providence deploys a two-pronged strategy in its attempt to reconcile the apparently contradictory facts that God is good, God is all-powerful, and evil happens. On one level it offloads responsibility for evil onto individual rational creatures (a category that includes both humans and angels), who misuse the divine gift of free will. Hence injustice and suffering is not God's fault, but stems from the free choices of creatures. Then, in response to the commonsense objection that God should not have allowed creaturely free will if he knew that it would lead to such bad results, the doctrine claims that God is able to draw good out of those evil choices, indeed a much greater good than would have been possible in a hypothetical evil-free creation. As Augustine puts it, tying in the aesthetic concerns that Taylor's genealogy highlights, the existence of evil enhances the beauty of creation, "as the beauty of a picture is increased by well-managed shadows."[25]

These two claims are obviously in tension. If our evil deeds actually enhance the beauty of God's creation—indeed, if they were, as the closely related doctrine of predestination maintains, very much part of the plan from the beginning—then why does God still punish us for them? The answer is that those deeds were freely chosen and hence morally blameworthy, regardless of whether God is able to derive some subsequent benefit from them. The determinative factor in God's judgment is not what we happen to achieve through our actions, which could be the result of contingent factors beyond our control. Rather, it is the condition of our free will that God is concerned with, specifically whether our will is in submission to the divine command. Doing something that God wants is not sufficient—after all, literally everything that happens in God's creation is ultimately what he wants to happen. Only an act of obedience that is *willed as such* is truly meritorious.

This connection between will or intention and moral judgment has deeply shaped the commonsense moral reasoning of the modern West. That profound influence makes it all the more disturbing to realize that in the Christian account of the will, at least in the form it had taken by the late medieval period, the emphasis falls overwhelming on the side of securing the blameworthiness of human actions, to the near-exclusion of any real consideration of moral achievement or merit. In the early centuries theologians could see in free will a sign of human dignity as being created in the image of God. Here Gregory of Nyssa, writing in the middle of the fourth century, is exemplary when he writes that God could not fail to provide us with "the most excellent and precious of blessings—I mean the gift of liberty and free will. For were human life governed by necessity, the 'image' would be falsified in that respect and so differ from the archetype. For how can a nature subject to necessity and in servitude be called an image of the sovereign nature?"[26] Over time, however, and particularly within the Latin West, theologians viewed free will less as a sign of harmonious likeness to the divine than as a site of potential rivalry and rebellion against God.

This suspicion of the will is expressed most forcefully in the doctrine of original sin, initially developed by Augustine, systematized by Scholastic theologians like Anselm of Canterbury and Thomas Aquinas, and then radicalized by the Protestant Reformers Luther and Calvin. For the sake of illustration I will take up Anselm's account,[27] which starts from the premise that every rational creature owes to God the submission of its will to God's commandment. As is well known, our first parents failed to show God the proper obedience, and the result was a distortion in their wills that was subsequently passed down to each of their descendants (§2). This distortion of the will means that human beings are born in a state of de facto rebellion against God, a condition that we cannot resolve on our own (§7). Yet despite the fact that this condition of the will has come about through no fault of the infant's own, it is nevertheless morally relevant precisely because it is a condition *of the will*, meaning that "all infants are equally unjust, because they have none of the justice which it is each man's duty to have" (§24). This injustice, this failure to live up to God's standards, is no less a sin than an obvious act of malice such as murder, and that means that every infant is born deserving to go to hell (§28). Thankfully, forgiveness of sin is available, which in Anselm's system takes the form of applying the superabundant merits of Jesus Christ (which he accumulated through willfully submitting to death) to the believer's debt of sin.[28] Once that forgiveness is achieved, the believer has some ability to begin acquiring merit, but that merit will always pale in comparison to Christ's merit, upon which it ultimately depends.

Not all of God's creatures are so fortunate. For the fallen angels—better known as demons—the free choice to rebel against God is permanent and irrevocable. This is above all the case for Satan or the devil, the angel who initiates the demonic rebellion and subsequently tempts humanity, setting in train literally every evil deed ever committed in God's good creation. The question of how the devil could ever turn against God presents a difficult conundrum, one that the theological tradition in the West seems strangely determined to exacerbate as much as possible. Early accounts provided the devil with something of a backstory, allowing for a comprehensible account of his motives. In the most common narrative, of which Gregory of Nyssa provides a well-known version,[29] the devil was appointed as a kind of guardian angel of earth, but gets wind of God's big plans for humans (who, as partly material beings, are clearly inferior to the purely spiritual angels in his opinion) and feels that his rightful position is threatened. Hence he conspires to seduce his human charges to keep them out of God's good graces. It is a story that certainly paints the devil in a bad light but nevertheless gives him familiar motives—wounded pride and status anxiety—that help to make sense of his malicious act in the Garden of Eden.

Later theologians increasingly rejected this story and, indeed, any recognizable narrative account whatsoever. Instead, they insisted, following Augustine, that the rebellious angels fell not only prior to the material creation, but as early as was logically possible—namely, the first instant after their creation.[30] Where the earlier story had envisioned an indefinite period of time prior to the devil's initial rebellion, Augustine claims that the devil "did not abide in the truth from the time of his own creation, and was accordingly never blessed with the holy angels," because he "refused to submit to his Creator" from the very beginning (11.13). We should not conclude from this, however, that "the devil has derived from some adverse evil principle a nature proper to himself" (11.13), because following the dictates of one's own nature is morally neutral: "if sin be natural, it is not sin at all" (11.15). Not nature but the will is the site of moral judgment, and the devil's will rejected the obligation to submit to God at the first available opportunity. Therefore, once again, God is not to blame for the devil's evil choice, since he created the devil with the capacity to submit to God's will. As punishment for their rebellion, the devil and his fellow demons are deprived of any ability to turn their will back toward God, but as with the hell-bound infant, this state of their will, which they cannot control or change, is nonetheless morally blameworthy precisely because it is the state *of their will.*

This conception of the fall of the devil is very difficult to understand. Everything that we associate with moral responsibility seems to be lacking. There is no moral obligation at play here other than sheer submission to God, a demand that seems to have no concrete content. There is no way to assess motivations or circumstances, because the decision to rebel was not only instantaneous but at the time it occurred was quite literally the only thing that had ever happened in God's created world. It seems more like a random impulse than a morally relevant choice, much less a choice carrying such severe and inescapable consequences. On this point, Augustine more or less agrees. When he asks what caused the demons to rebel while the other angels stood firm, he is forced to conclude that there is no discernible reason for this difference: "However minutely we examine the case . . . , we can discern nothing which caused the will of the one to be evil" (12.6). In short, an arbitrary, instantaneous demand elicits an equally arbitrary response.

On some formal level the demons had the freedom to choose "rightly," as illustrated by the fact that some of their peers in fact did so. Yet their agency appears so small as to be meaningless, especially seeing that God holds all the cards here, since he did, after all, create all these angels out of nothing and could foresee precisely what they would do. It is difficult not to conclude that God is setting them up to fall specifically so that he can blame and punish them. This cuts against a commonsense reading of the doctrine of providence, namely that God allows evil to happen owing to the conceptual necessity of allowing free will and subsequently makes up for it by drawing good out of evil. What the primal scene of the fall of the devil shows is that the causation is reversed: the first thing God does is induce some of his creatures to "rebel" against a meaningless imperious demand, to ensure that there will be a reservoir of evil for him to turn toward the greater good.

In everyday language we tend to use the term *demonization* to refer to hyperbolic accusations or insults. I want to suggest that this detour through the Christian tradition provides us with a more precise sense of what it means to "demonize" someone. To "demonize" is to set someone up to fall, providing them with just the barest sliver of agency necessary to render them blameworthy. This is how the theological tradition envisions the process by which God produces demons, a strategy that he then repeats in order to entrap his human subjects into a debt of sin—all for his greater glory.

If God's first move after creating the world is to secure the existence of evil by demonizing the rebellious angels, then that means that the paradigm of providence is necessarily tied up with the dynamics of demonization. My argument in this chapter is that the same applies to the secularized providence of the self-regulating market. This is so because both the openly theological and the ostensibly secular version of providence depend precisely on drawing good out of our *negative* inclinations: in theological terms our sinfulness and lust of the flesh, in secular terms our selfish and base material desires. The virtue of the invisible hand is that it is able to take our specifically *self-interested* choices and harmonize them into social good.

Yet the providential hand of the market, like its divine model, is not content simply to wait around for us to make selfish decisions. It must force us to be selfish in the particular way it demands, which means seeking open-ended material gain. Any impulse to seek the social good directly, apart from the grace of the market, must be stifled. For the wealthy, ideological discourse is often sufficient, while for the workers themselves, a more powerful form of persuasion is required—namely, the ever-present threat of starvation, which the ideologues of early capitalism publicly and explicitly promoted as a tool of public policy.[31] If the workers cannot see their own self-interest, then it must be made inescapably clear.

The Market in Demonization

The alliance between capitalism (in its classical and neoliberal versions) and reactionary Christianity is founded in the indissoluble link between providence and demonization. The difference between the (neo)liberal and (neo)conservative approaches is primarily one of emphasis. Whereas (neo)liberals deploy the tool of demonization for the sake of maintaining the secular providential machine, (neo)conservatives have recourse to providence as a way of justifying their ever more hyperbolic demonization. After all, if the doctrine of providence emerged as a way to explain the existence of evil, the confrontation with the kind of sheer malevolent malice that the *Malleus Maleficarum* attributes to witches, for instance, necessarily kicks the providential apparatus into overdrive. Indeed, the first book of that infamous text is taken up with an extended, and surprisingly theologically rigorous, discussion of the providential implications of the witches' supposed campaign of terror against Christendom.

Neither group seriously disputes that divine favor (as they construe it) is displayed through worldly power and prosperity. Where disagreements arise, they center primarily on the degree of demonization. Demonization in the strictest sense occurs only in the fall of the devil and his demons: an instantaneous and irreversible descent into evil, for which no redemption is possible. Yet what happens to human beings under the sway of original sin is not different in kind so much as in degree. Sinful humans start out, like the demons, in a state of moral dereliction from the very first moment of their existence, but unlike the demons, they have the opportunity to benefit from the divine economy of salvation. We can say, then, that original sin imposes on human beings a conditional demonization, in contrast to the absolute demonization experienced by the fallen angels.

Broadly speaking, the (neo)conservative is more comfortable with the gesture of absolute demonization, whereas the (neo)liberal is more open to the possibility of redemption. To use a contemporary example, reactionary Christians regard homosexuals as beyond the pale, whereas neoliberals are open to the possibility of allowing them to participate in family life and the

wealth acquisition that it entails. The difference is that between demanding a degree of total repentance that homosexuals experience as absolutely
impossible and making room for a choice to practice homosexuality in a "responsible" (monogamous, family-oriented) way. It is worth reflecting here
on the extent to which this debate between neoconservatives and neoliberals
hinges on the question of whether homosexuality is a "choice." Where neoconservatives insist, as is required by their view that homosexuality is morally
culpable, that homosexuality is in fact a choice, neoliberals view it as an intrinsic quality of the person and hence as not morally relevant per se—the
only ground for moral judgment is how homosexuals express their sexual
orientation, specifically whether they are able to embed their homosexual
practice in a stable family life.

Completely missing from the mainstream debate is the idea that homosexuality is a choice and that choosing it—including the nonnormative
sexual and kinship practices it has entailed—would be morally salutary. Indeed, that position was explicitly rejected during the AIDS crisis when, as
Cooper documents, neoliberals opposed any publicly funded effort to combat a crisis that they viewed as the result of freely chosen risky behavior.
Using language familiar to students of the recent Global Financial Crisis,
they viewed the problem presented by the AIDS crisis "as one of 'moral haz-
ard': When the state subsidizes health care for those who have voluntarily
assumed the risks of infection, it ends up lowering the price of high-risk
behavior and endorsing irresponsible lifestyle choices such as promiscuity or
addiction."[32] From the neoliberal perspective, "social insurance . . . actively
discourages the classical liberal virtues of prudence and self-care by subsidiz-
ing the costs of high-risk behavior,"[33] and so "to counteract the social costs
of unsafe sex, they argue, the state would do well to limit its interventions to
promoting marriage."[34]

The question of free will, so central to the Christian moral order, is
equally crucial for neoliberal morality. This is so at a literal level: "*Volenti non
fit injuria*"—to the willing person no wrong can be done—"is the legal translation of the idea that risk, once consented to, must be borne entirely by the
individual, unless one can prove fraud or duress in the performance of a contract."[35] One does not normally associate the decision to have sex with the
kind of reasoned deliberation necessary for entering into a legally binding

contract. But just as the fallen angels' arbitrary impulse of resistance against God was interpreted as a morally relevant act of rebellion, so too from the neoliberal perspective is every decision, even the most impulsive and impassioned, treated as a reasoned attempt at utility maximization.

A particularly clear account of this moral outlook can be found in Gary Becker's Nobel Lecture, entitled "The Economic Way of Looking at Behavior."[36] To characterize this text as a moral treatise may seem strange. First of all, he is quite insistent that his goal is the purely methodological one of providing ways "to analyze social issues that range beyond those usually considered by economists." And the first step in developing that broader approach is to distance himself from the idea "that individuals are motivated solely by selfishness of material gain" (385). In Becker's view, "Behavior is driven by a much richer set of values and preferences," and we should limit ourselves to assuming "that individuals maximize welfare *as they conceive it*, whether they be selfish, altruistic, loyal, spiteful, or masochistic" (385–86; emphasis in original).

Becker's first two examples fit with his reputation for amoral thought experiments, as he attempts to construe first racial discrimination and then criminal activity as rational choices. In the first case, taking for granted that some people have racist preferences, Becker argues that such preferences may not be absolute and hence could be offset by higher costs in other areas—whether through legal sanction in the case of antidiscrimination laws or through the less direct path of providing high-quality job training to minorities to make their value as employees outweigh the benefit the racist believes he derives from discriminating against them. In other words, the goal of public policy should be to figure out how much racial discrimination is really worth to people and then either make it unaffordable or else make nondiscrimination too profitable to pass up.

The idea of solving racism by buying off the racists is hardly an edifying thought, and at first glance, neither is Becker's account of crime as a matter of coldly weighing the pros and cons of breaking the law. Nevertheless, he believes that his view is preferable to the prevailing opinion in the 1950s and 1960s that "criminal behavior was caused by mental illness and social oppression, and that criminals were helpless 'victims.'" For his part, Becker reports that he "was not sympathetic to the assumption that criminals had radically different motivations from everyone else. I explored instead the theoretical and empirical implications of the assumption that criminal behavior is rational" (390). Though he does not dwell on it, one can detect an unexpected concern for the human dignity of criminals. They are not incomprehensible demons, trapped forever in irrational patterns of destructive behavior, nor are they automatons of fate. They are rational human beings just like Gary Becker, who himself confesses to committing the minor crime of parking illegally after calculating that the risk was likely worth the benefit (389). And he advocates an approach to crime that is as rational as Becker's fellow criminals are, balancing costs and benefits without getting caught up in an emotional desire for retaliation and punishment.

This facade of moral neutrality begins to crack during his discussion of the family. Becker is amusingly cynical at times, most notably in his account of familial emotional manipulation as an economic strategy. Yet it is clear that his goal is to protect and promote some version of traditional family life and that he is primarily concerned with how to use public policy to foster intimate family relationships. Crucial to his discussion is the question of elder care, which he believes to be a major motivating factor in parents' strategies to cultivate their children's sense of affection and obligation (or else bribe them with the promise of a bequest). From his perspective, "programs such as social security that significantly help the elderly would encourage family members to drift apart emotionally, not by accident but as maximizing responses to those policies." More generally, beneficial phenomena like "increased geographical mobility, the greater wealth that comes with economic growth, better capital and insurance markets, higher divorce rates, smaller families, and publicly funded health care" have "weakened the personal relations within families between husbands and wives, parents and children, and among more distant relatives, partly by reducing the incentives to invest in *creating* closer relations" (401; emphasis in original). It is only a short step from this analysis to the perceived necessity to eliminate welfare protections—precisely to force people into a position where they will choose freely and rationally to cultivate strong family relationships.

In theological terms, Becker's analyses of crime and the family both point toward a kind of secularized grace, whereby the providential hand of the state sets up the economy in a way that "nudges" the individual toward righteousness.[37] Yet this hopeful face of neoliberalism is inextricably tied up with the kind of callous abandonment of entire populations that we have seen in the neoliberal response to the AIDS crisis. For a privileged few, the providential economy of "nudges" allows them to begin accumulating merit. But for the majority of the population, the experience is that of demonization: the assumption of rational choice in the absence of meaningful agency generates only blameworthiness. Neoliberalism makes demons of us all.

The Neoliberal Inferno

This shadow side of the neoliberal concept of free choice grows naturally out of the fact that, as Brown points out, neoliberalism emphasizes not market exchange (which presupposes equality) but market competition (which necessarily entails inequality, since there must be winners and losers).[38] And as the insistence on family shows, this competition is not purely individual but can involve larger groupings. Most accounts of neoliberalism emphasize competition on the geographic and political level, in which units ranging from the state (or superstate in the case of the European Union) down to the individual city and even neighborhood compete for capital and the jobs it can bring to their constituencies. Yet the importance of the family points in another direction, toward groupings defined by sexual practice (such as AIDS patients, as they were reductively envisioned in the mainstream media) or by racial descent. For gay men who "choose" to expose themselves to AIDS, as for black men who "choose" not to display the impossible level of instant abject submission demanded by police, the presumption of freedom becomes a trap that leaves them either abandoned to death or actively murdered—not on the basis of the individual's own unique circumstances but on the authorities' ostensibly "reasonable" reliance on stereotypes to increase efficiency in issuing their judgments.

Despite a formal commitment to nondiscrimination and "color blindness," neoliberalism institutes a competition among sexualities and racialized groups, not just individuals, firms, and political units. In this competition, historically dominant groups certainly have an advantage, but minority groups can find a niche—as in the widespread perception of Americans of East Asian descent as a "model minority" with a special gift for meritocratic climbing, or the increasing acceptance of monogamous gay and lesbian couples. Yet this competition produces losers as well, such as blacks and members of sexual minorities that fit less easily into the template of the traditional family (e.g., transgender and other gender nonconforming people). Individual success stories may arise within disadvantaged groups—think of the rapid political ascent of Barack Obama, for instance, or the favorable media coverage of the transgender television personality Caitlyn Jenner in the wake of her transition—but the groups as a whole are exposed to deprivation, economic exploitation, and violence. And to add insult to injury, the social order alternates between declaring their plight a deserved result of morally culpable decisions and congratulating itself for generously providing opportunities for individuals to succeed despite their background.

No book has documented these dynamics as well as Michelle Alexander's *The New Jim Crow*.[39] Her argument that the War on Drugs and mass incarceration have emerged as the latest way to maintain America's racial caste system is as influential as it is devastating. It has awakened a new awareness of systemic racism in a society that had come to regard itself as "color blind" or "postracial," and it has brought into the mainstream debate the radical claim that the prison system needs to be not simply reformed but completely abolished. While Alexander does not explicitly position her work with respect to neoliberalism, the evidence she accumulates points inescapably toward the conclusion that we are dealing not only with a New, but with a distinctively Neoliberal, Jim Crow.

On the level of explicit public policy, for instance, she makes it clear that Reagan's goal of radically stepping up the enforcement of drug laws, a move that few states and municipalities supported when it was first proposed, was achieved not primarily through direct legal mandates but through financial incentives for police departments, which also gained the opportunity to use asset seizures as a profit center. It is hard to imagine a more literal response to the neoliberal imperative that government should be run like a business. Just as with the neoliberal approach to AIDS, the crack epidemic was viewed not as a public health crisis but as a question of culpable choices whose perpetrators must be made to bear the costs. This led to a massive increase in law enforcement and prison funding, while by contrast, the budget for the National Institute on Drug Abuse and for antidrug education programs were both cut by approximately 80 percent during Reagan's first term (49–50).

The media storm that followed can only be described as a demonization campaign aimed at black communities most afflicted by the so-called demon drug: "Thousands of stories about the crack crisis flooded the airwaves and newsstands, and the stories had a clear racial subtext. The articles typically featured black 'crack whores,' 'crack babies,' and 'gangbangers,' reinforcing already prevalent racial stereotypes of black women as irresponsible, selfish 'welfare queens,' and black men as 'predators'—part of an inferior and criminal subculture" (52). The figure of the "crack baby" is especially poignant from the theological perspective, because it envisions black children as born with a preexisting addiction to the very drug that was supposedly turning their parents into uncontrollable criminals—an uncanny parallel to the inborn distortion of the will caused by original sin. More broadly, the view that crack was irresistible once taken renders drug addicts, like the fallen angels, simultaneously irredeemable and morally responsible, since their condition results from their ostensibly free choice to take crack rather than "just say no."

Some of the most upsetting passages in *The New Jim Crow* detail the ways that police attempt to draw even innocent or marginally involved people into the realm of criminal justice. Their techniques can almost all be characterized as forms of entrapment, designed to force people to "freely" confess to criminal wrongdoing. The anecdote with which she opens the book's third chapter, "The Color of Justice," is particularly outrageous:

> Imagine you are Erma Faye Stewart, a thirty-year-old, single African American mother of two who was arrested as part of a drug sweep in Hearne, Texas. All but one of the people arrested were African American. You are innocent. After a week in jail, you have no one to care for your two small children and are eager to get home. Your court-appointed attorney urges you to plead guilty to a drug distribution charge, saying the prosecutor has offered probation. You refuse, steadfastly proclaiming your innocence. Finally, after almost a month in jail, you decide to plead guilty so you can return home to your children. (97)

Here we are dealing with literal criminalization: as a result of this spurious, extorted confession, she is "branded a felon" despite being factually innocent of any crime. The only thing that makes her a criminal is her having been induced to say that she was. As a result of this purely notional status, she is ordered to pay a massive fine, deprived of welfare benefits (including public housing, leading to homelessness), and stripped of employment discrimination protections and voting rights. Worst of all, the case in which she was swept up is ultimately dismissed, but she is still on the books as a felon because she confessed—freely, of course. This is an extreme case of entrapment, but Alexander documents widespread patterns in which police are able to seize on any action—including minor traffic violations or simply appearing suspicious in some way—as a pretext to subject blacks to searches that would otherwise be illegal, increasing their odds of being incriminated.

This campaign of demonization and entrapment appears even more cruel and gratuitous when one recognizes that "people of all colors *use and sell* illegal drugs at remarkably similar rates" and that at the time the drug war was declared, "drug crime was declining, not rising" (7; emphasis in original). As Alexander notes, "Sociologists have frequently pointed out that governments use punishment primarily as a tool of social control, and thus the extent or severity of punishment is often unrelated to actual crime patterns. Michael Tonry explains in *Thinking About Crime*: 'Governments decide how much punishment they want, and these decisions are in no simple way related to crime rates'" (7). Just as God needed a certain level of evil rebellion and set about inciting it, so too did the Reagan administration need a certain level of black criminality and set about creating it. In both cases the vagaries of free choice constituted the raw material out of which the demons could be crafted, and in both cases, the newly minted demons play a crucial role in legitimating the ruler. Reagan and the elder Bush both benefited from their ability to signal that they were forcefully putting blacks in their place while maintaining the plausible deniability of an ostensibly nonracial basis for doing so. For their part, Clinton and Obama were able to present substantively identical policies as an attempt to help black communities by freeing them of criminals, just as they could position welfare cuts as a bid to end dependency and thereby enhance black people's dignity and self-esteem. The difference is one of emphasis rather than substance, with the neoconservatives favoring demonization and the neoliberals focusing on the possibility of redemption.

Criminalization and incarceration are the most extreme consequences of losing out in the tacit competition that neoliberalism institutes between the racialized groups. The prison system, moreover, is still very much a part of the neoliberal order. Not only do local communities compete to host prisons (and the jobs they carry with them), but in the United States the early 2000s saw a privatization wave in even this seemingly most central state function. Nor is it just a matter of warehousing prisoners for the sake of job creation and corporate profit: incarcerated workers can also be made available to private enterprises eager to cut labor costs, as the Thirteenth Amendment abolished slavery in all cases except as a legal punishment.

Back home, poverty and criminalization depress property values in black neighborhoods, making them ripe targets for urban gentrification or for predatory slumlords and payday lenders. The latter possibilities are particularly vivid illustrations of the neoliberal ethos of competition, where contracts are not an agreement between equals seeking mutual benefit so much as a calculated risk in the never-ending quest to accumulate both monetary and social capital. Hence punitive interest rates or unfair lease agreements are not an injustice perpetrated on the victims, but must be viewed as risks that they freely took on. By the same token, whatever profit can be extracted from them represents not exploitation, but an obligation freely entered into. Just as the state receives the glory of legitimacy for being "tough on crime"—either to punish blacks or uplift them, as the occasion demands—so too does the economy derive glorious surplus value from those who have been entrapped in neoliberalism's version of hell.[40]

The same dynamics of entrapment and predatory lending play out in the grand competition for capital that neoliberalism institutes on an international scale. It is well-known that the International Monetary Fund and World Bank have frequently imposed the strictures of the Washington Consensus on countries that were desperate for credit, leading to "structural adjustment" policies that often left them unable to service their debt—prompting another round of loans and another round of austerity and privatization. This is a very concrete way in which neoliberalism does, as Wendy Brown contends, hollow out democracy, by directly constraining democratically elected governments to implement policies that they have "freely" agreed to follow. The same happens within countries, as regional and municipal governments are forced to embrace neoliberal "best practices" to maintain "competitiveness" or else face capital flight and mass immiseration.

Some of the most potent conflicts in the neoliberal order happen where geographic and racial competition overlap—namely, outsourcing and immigration. The relationship between the United States and Mexico is exemplary here, as Mexico is envisioned as "stealing" American jobs in both directions, first by tempting American companies into relocating and then by sending migrant workers who habitually underbid and outwork their American counterparts. This is also a site of conflict between neoconservative and neoliberal forces, in which the latter emphasize the hard work and meritocratic striving of Latino immigrants, while the former attempt to demonize all Latinos as criminals by association with undocumented (or "illegal") immigrants or, more broadly, as an inassimilable foreign element. Just as with the conflict over gay marriage, both sides agree on the broadly conservative goal of assimilation but differ on the extent to which it is possible.

The US-Mexico example is particularly interesting for our purposes because the United States has had a large population of Mexican descent virtually from the time of the Founding—indeed, large regions of US territory were at one time part of Mexico—and migrant labor from Latin America has been an integral part of the US agricultural system for generations. The specific relationship between the United States and Mexico imagined by mainstream American political discourse is therefore not the result of a sudden influx of Mexicans where previously there were none, nor does it represent some "leftover" element of racial animus toward Latin Americans that neoliberal politicians are opportunistically indulging. This conflictual relationship arose during the neoliberal era, as a direct result of the neoliberal restructuring of the US economy through deindustrialization and free trade. To the extent that it draws on a well of preexisting racism, the neoliberal situation has reconfigured that racism into a new and distinctly neoliberal form—just as it has done with white Americans' more severe and durable racism against blacks.

Hence the "double movement" hypothesis, no less than the political-economic dichotomy, needs to be set aside. Neoliberalism is a social order, which means that it is an order of family and sexuality and an order of racial hierarchy and subordination. It is a political order, which means that it is an order of law and punishment and an order of war and international relations. And it is above all a remarkably cohesive moral order, deploying the same logic of constrained agency (demonization), competition (in which there must be both winners and losers), and conformity ("best practices") at every level: from the individual to the household to the racial grouping to the region to the country to the world.

Neoliberalism is, in sum, a totalizing world order, an integral self-reinforcing system of political theology, and it has progressively transformed our world into a living hell. This is felt most acutely by those who have been fully demonized by an economically rapacious and brutally violent prison system. From a political theological perspective, we can see that this infernal system is far from being some merely particular "issue" or "cause"—it is the most extreme expression of the logic of our neoliberal order. The rest of those of us excluded from the elect 1 percent are not so thoroughly demonized, but our lives are increasingly hemmed in by a logic of entrapment and victim-blaming. The psychic life of neoliberalism, as so memorably characterized by Mark Fisher in *Capitalist Realism*, is shot through with anxiety and shame. We have to be in a constant state of high alert, always "hustling" for opportunities and connections, always planning for every contingency (including the inherently unpredictable vagaries of health and longevity). This dynamic of "responsibilization," as Wendy Brown calls it, requires us to fritter away our life with worry and paperwork and supplication, "pitching" ourselves over and over again, building our "personal brand"—all for ever-lowering wages or a smattering of piece-work, which barely covers increasingly exorbitant rent, much less student loan payments.

The vulgar libertarianism that neoliberalism presents as its public face is an integral part of this victim-blaming dynamic. Its atomistic individualism attempts to cover up the existence of systemic forces beyond any individual's control. Its naturalization of the invisible hand of the market and rejection of the meddling influence of the state combine to obscure the fact that the economy is not a realm of unrestrained freedom but of governance and control—one that has been intentionally constructed in a certain way by human beings who, as Mirowski forcefully points out, can often be named individually. Libertarianism does not describe the actual workings of the neoliberal economy, but it does perfectly capture its moral dynamic of using freedom as a mechanism to generate blameworthiness. If you fail, it is your fault, and yours alone. You are in control of your destiny, and if your destiny is miserable, then misery must be what you deserve, because the market is always right. If Job's friends were alive today, they would be libertarians.

This dynamic of demonization entraps us emotionally. If we buy into the narrative of personal responsibility and agency, then our financial insecurity and underemployment must be our own fault—leading to a feeling of shame when we prove persistently unable to overcome them. If we recognize the systemic forces at work, it can be difficult to avoid a feeling of utter despair. And meanwhile, not even the system's ostensible beneficiaries seem to be enjoying themselves, as our ruling classes—most notably the billionaire who has reached the pinnacle of power and fame—continually complain of being unappreciated and unfairly attacked.

The neoliberal order increasingly spreads only misery, but in this very misery there may be a paradoxical glimmer of hope. Even though there really is no "leftover" institutional form that automatically escapes the logic of neoliberalism, there are still desires and demands—including among those, such as myself, who have known nothing but the neoliberal order for our entire lives—that reject it and potentially exceed it. Already, those desires and demands are beginning to place a major strain on the neoliberal order. The question that remains for us is whether they can be harnessed to form a genuine alternative. As the next chapter will show, the early indications are mixed at best.

CHAPTER 4

THIS PRESENT DARKNESS

In 1989 Francis Fukuyama published an essay entitled "The End of History?"[1] Though the 1992 book-length version of the argument is better-known, the shorter essay is an interesting document in its own right. Coming before the fall of the Berlin Wall (which would happen in November of that year), much less the dissolution of the Soviet Union itself (which would endure through 1991), it is more cautious than one would expect from the book's subsequent reputation. Where the latter appeared in the context of triumphalism, as Americans came to believe that they had "won" the Cold War, the shorter essay focuses more on "the total exhaustion of viable systematic alternatives to Western liberalism." On the basis of this ambiguous victory in an ideological war of attrition, Fukuyama claims that "we may be witnessing . . . the end point of mankind's ideological evolution and the universalization of Western liberal democracy as the final form of human government" (1).

This one-sided emphasis on liberal democracy as a political ideal is strange, given the primary evidence Fukuyama adduces for the global triumph of Western thought is precisely the spread of Western commercial culture: experimentation with markets in the Soviet Union, the popularity of Western classical music in Japan, "and the rock music enjoyed alike in Prague, Rangoon, and Tehran." And though he attempts to obscure it somewhat through his idiosyncratic descriptions, the narrative arc he supplies

for the twentieth century is one in which politics and economics are deeply
intertwined:

> The twentieth century saw the developed world descend into a paroxysm of
> ideological violence, as liberalism contended first with the remnants of abso-
> lutism, then bolshevism [*sic*] and fascism, and finally to an updated Marxism
> that threatened to lead to the ultimate apocalypse of nuclear war. But the
> century that began full of self-confidence in the ultimate triumph of Western
> liberal democracy seems at its close to be returning full circle to where it
> started: not to an "end of ideology" or a convergence between capitalism and
> socialism, as earlier predicted, but to an unabashed victory of economic and
> political liberalism. (1)

In terms of the main events, this is a narrative that critics and exponents of
neoliberalism would recognize. Yet both would equally object to the idea
that "economic and political liberalism" was somehow passively waiting for
the various alternatives to exhaust themselves. As we have seen, the return
to a new version of classical liberalism at the end of the twentieth century
was not the simple reemergence of something that had always been lurking in the background but the result of an aggressive political movement.
Fukuyama knows this very well, because he had not only witnessed that
transformation—as a member of the Reagan administration, he actively
participated in it.

Hence Marika Rose is right to connect Fukuyama's "end of history" thesis
to the triumph not of liberal democratic political institutions but of neoliberalism.[2] And Fukuyama is actively contributing to the "end of history" that
he claims to be documenting, insofar as he is hard at work naturalizing neoliberalism as what is left over once its ideological opponents have exhausted
themselves. From this perspective his argument marks a turning point in the
history of the neoliberal "end of history," the shift, in Will Davies's terms,
from "combative neoliberalism" to "normative neoliberalism."[3] The former
period, which Davies defines as lasting from 1979 through 1989, was the
Reagan-Thatcher era, when neoliberalism "was a self-conscious insurgency,
a social movement aimed at combating and ideally destroying the enemies
of liberal capitalism" (126). The latter, ranging from 1989 to 2008, was the
era when ostensibly progressive parties took the lead, responding to the new

political terrain in which "a single political-economic system" had emerged victorious by embracing the "explicitly normative" project of "how to render that system 'fair'" (127).

In retrospect, the 1990s and early 2000s were the classical era of neoliberalism, the period when the project shifted from its one-sidedly polemical emphasis toward a more positive and constructive stance. Embracing the ethos of omnipresent competition, center-left neoliberals like Clinton and Blair attempted "to ensure that 'winners' were clearly distinguishable from 'losers,' and that the contest was perceived as fair" (127). Under normative neoliberalism "neoclassical economics becomes a soft constitution for government, or 'governance' in its devolved forms. Normative questions of fairness, reward, and recognition become channeled into economic tests of efficiency and comparisons of 'excellence.' Coupled to markets and quasi-market contests, the ideal is that of meritocracy, of reward being legitimately earned, rather than arbitrarily inherited" (128). In other words, where the combative stage had been content to secure the actual victory of neoliberalism, the normative stage undertook to legitimate it. And they were largely successful, as rising income inequality did not become a major political issue as long as economic growth continued and the various economic and quasi-market testing regimes appeared to be fair and evenhanded. The mantra of "there is no alternative"—which under Thatcher and Reagan had been at once an aspiration and a threat—fell aside as meritocratic metrics took on an "*a priori* status" throughout all levels of society. Only with the Global Financial Crisis was the spell truly broken, when "it emerged that systems of audit and economic modeling could potentially serve vested political and economic interests." This means that massive income inequality, "which had been rising in most of the Global North since the 1980s, returned as a major concern only once the tests of legitimate inequality had been found to be faulty" (129).

In the wake of the crisis, Davies believes we moved into a new stage: punitive neoliberalism. Where normative neoliberalism had witnessed an explosion of credit at every level, justified as a motor for creating economic opportunity, punitive neoliberalism marks the moment when the bill comes due: "The transfer of banking debts onto government balance sheets, creating the justification for austerity, has triggered a third phase of neoliberalism, which operates with an ethos of heavily moralized—as opposed to utilitarian—punishment. What distinguishes the spirit of punishment is its *post jure* logic, that is, the sense that the moment of judgment has already passed, and questions of value or guilt are no longer open to deliberation" (130). As Rose points out, this is the "end of history" with a vengeance: a Last Judgment that consigns us all to the hell of eternal indebtedness. Here Agamben's vision of the hellishness of modernity's eternal economizing is horrifically overlain with Christian eschatology—the ultimate synthesis of providential neoliberalism and demonizing neoconservatism. Under this regime, public policy takes increasingly punitive forms that in terms of "most standards of orthodox economic evaluation . . . are self-destructive." The overall ethos is one of retribution, driven by "the sense that we 'deserve' to suffer for credit-fuelled economic growth" (130). "There is no alternative" does not name a project—whether the negative one of tearing down public institutions or the positive one of constructing elaborate artificial markets—so much as the absolute trump card that silences all debate and dissent. Davies quotes former Greek Finance Minister Yanis Varoufakis's description of his experience negotiating the terms of his country's debt as exemplary: "You put forward an argument that you've really worked on—to make sure it's logically coherent—and you're just faced with blank stares. It's as if you haven't spoken" (121).

Aside from the intrinsic interest of his analysis, what makes Davies's piece so valuable for thinking through our present is the perspective he brings. I mean this in two senses. First, he is writing before the twin shocks of 2016: the Brexit vote and the cruel Electoral College technicality that led to the Trump presidency.[4] Second, he is writing from a British perspective, meaning that "punitive neoliberalism" had clearly been in force long before 2016. With Davies's periodization in mind we can see that Obama represented a failed attempt to salvage normative neoliberalism in the United States. Seemingly through sheer force of personal charisma, he was able to maintain the presidency for two terms, allowing him to expand health care access along normative neoliberal lines and subsequently to restrain the worst excesses of the more clearly punitive neoliberalism espoused by Tea Party Republicans. At every level of government below the presidency, however, punitive neoliberalism made more and more gains with every election, creating a situation in which the Republicans could come close enough to winning the popular vote to seize the presidency.

If we follow Melinda Cooper in viewing the neoliberal era as defined by the alliance between neoconservatives and neoliberals, then Davies's periodization could look like a cycle in which each partner takes turns leading the way. In terms of my analysis, that alternation would correspond to a greater focus on either demonization (neoconservatives) or the providential opportunity for redemption (neoliberals). Within such a scheme, our present moment could be interpreted as "normal" in the broad run of things, and we may even allow ourselves to hope that the current neoconservative phase will be succeeded by a new Obama-style "neoliberalism with a human face."

What such a vision of alternating emphases misses, however, is that the overlap between neoliberals and neoconservatives was never complete. On the one hand, a vocal minority of neoconservatives has always rejected the basic legitimacy of their neoliberal partners and thoroughly demonized them. In the United States one thinks of the Clinton impeachment and the "Birther" conspiracy theory that claimed Obama was not even a US citizen and, in the United Kingdom, of the scapegoating of the European Union and the immigrants it brought with it. Both Clinton and Obama were happy to forge bipartisan deals with the neoconservatives who sought to annihilate them, just as New Labour was eager to listen to "legitimate concerns" around immigration, even as the neoconservatives grew ever more implacable and demanding. On the other hand, the traditionally progressive parties that neoliberals used as a flag of convenience still housed a remnant faithful to the Fordist social welfare state (such as Bernie Sanders and Jeremy Corbyn), who have skillfully exploited unexpected opportunities and thereby reintroduced pre-neoliberal values into the public debate. As these tensions have grown more and more unmanageable, we seem to have entered new terrain, where the spell of "there is no alternative" has been broken. Whereas for an entire generation it was impossible to vote against the neoliberal consensus, now we are witnessing the emergence of political leaders who explicitly reject neoliberalism.

Is this the end of neoliberalism? In this chapter and the conclusion that follows, I will not attempt to answer this question in any straightforward way. Instead, I will seek to interrogate the question itself using the tools of political theology that I have developed so far. This means asking what it might mean for neoliberalism to end and how we could tell if a genuine alternative were taking form, rather than merely a new variation on the theme. Naturally, I will be largely (though not exclusively) concerned with analyzing the present political conjuncture. My primary focus will be the debacle unfolding in the United States, as that is the setting where the reactionary wave has most directly taken power so far. This chapter was initially drafted in the summer of 2017, when there were seemingly daily revelations surrounding the Trump-Russia connection and UK politics took on an increasingly surreal tone with Teresa May's ill-fated snap election. Rather than update it with later news events that will seem almost equally dated by the time this book is ultimately published, I have chosen to limit my examples to events from that baffling period of time. I hope the reader will forgive the out-of-date references, in recognition of the fact that my aim in this chapter is neither journalistic nor predictive, but diagnostic and retrospective. Rather than trying to guess at the outcome of a confusing political moment, I will be treating the unexpected and often quite disturbing political forces that have emerged in recent years as a source of new information about neoliberalism's weaknesses and internal contradictions as a political-theological paradigm.

I Wish We'd All Been Ready

The immediate aftermath of the 2008 Global Financial Crisis is arguably the last time that the alliance between neoliberals and neoconservatives was fully functional in the United States. Though the Democrats, who by then controlled Congress, required some coaxing—Treasury Secretary Hank Paulson "literally bent down on one knee" to beg House Speaker Nancy Pelosi to support the bill,[5] which ultimately passed only after an initial failed vote caused a stock market crash—in the end both sides of the alliance (represented roughly by the two major political parties) came together to pass and implement the bailout policy. In what was reportedly one of the smoothest presidential transitions in history, outgoing Bush officials worked closely with their incoming Obama administration counterparts to administer the largest financial-sector bailout ever seen. And as I pointed out in my first chapter, it all proceeded according to neoliberal chapter and verse. The US bailouts ultimately solved the massive market failure by injecting funds into all major players, in a way designed to minimize state influence over each firm's internal decision making, while turning a modest profit for the US Treasury.

Yet despite the studious avoidance of direct state control over the major banks, the period immediately following the crisis was also the point when the illusion of a clear separation between state and economy—so crucial for neoliberalism's attempt to naturalize the economic order it had installed— began to break down. Even the most casual observer could recognize that for the first several years after the crisis, financial markets moved primarily in response to central bank pronouncements on monetary policy rather than any purely economic trends. And on the fiscal policy side, the ideas of John Maynard Keynes, so crucial to the development of the postwar Fordist order that neoliberalism had dismantled, enjoyed a brief vogue as economists argued that government deficit spending could boost economic output overall. This led to the passage of the relatively modest stimulus bill, which consisted primarily in accelerating the funding for already-approved projects and was the last major Obama initiative to enjoy any support from Republicans. By the time he turned to health care reform—starting with a template developed by conservative think tanks and implemented at the state level by the Republican Mitt Romney when he was governor of Massachusetts—the Republicans began the program of unrelenting opposition and obstruction that would characterize the remainder of Obama's presidency.

What went wrong? Though there was significant public outrage related to the bank bailouts, particularly after bailed-out firms paid bonuses to their employees despite having caused a world-historical economic downturn, political elites were largely unresponsive to such concerns. The problem was not the bailouts or even the economic downturn as such. The neoliberal era had seen its share of both, and none had seriously called the legitimacy of the system into question. What made this crisis different was that it was so intimately tied up with the household and hence raised profound questions of legitimacy.

As Cooper has shown, what Davies calls combative neoliberalism came to power in part through its skillful manipulation of anxieties surrounding family structure, crafting a narrative that reinterpreted the economic crisis of the late 1970s as a reflection of a moral crisis that had thrown gender roles, sexual norms, and racial hierarchies into disarray. Less than a month after Obama's inauguration, a similar narrative began to crystallize around an odd political rant delivered from the floor of the Chicago Board of Trade by the stock trader Rick Santelli, during a segment on the business news network CNBC. Castigating the government policies that he believed would reward the "losers" who had freely chosen to buy houses they could not afford, Santelli called for a "Chicago Tea Party" to protest the state's refusal to let people bear the consequences of their actions.[6]

This was certainly a counterintuitive setting and messenger for the Tea Party movement, at least if we accept the identification of that movement as "populist." It makes perfect sense, however, if we view Santelli as expressing the intuitions behind Davies's punitive neoliberalism, over against Obama's attempt to extend the normative neoliberal era. This conflict could be couched as a dispute within the neoliberal side of the alliance, insofar as, at least in its early days, the Tea Party was normally viewed as jettisoning the religiously inflected "culture wars" baggage of neoconservatism in favor of a more principled libertarian noninterventionism. Yet already in Santelli's rant we can see that the real emphasis was not on economic policy or GDP growth, but on making sure that people suffer for making bad choices. That is to say, the debate was not primarily economic but moral—and the specific inflection of that morality fit with the neoconservative tendency toward demonization rather than the neoliberal rhetoric of redemption through equality of opportunity.

As in the early days of combative neoliberalism, this moral discourse was also a racial discourse. The problem for the Tea Party was not merely that "losers" had unaccountably decided to get mortgages they could not afford, but specifically that ostensibly undeserving members of racial minorities had received government support for their financial largess. The Community Reinvestment Act (CRA), which outlawed discrimination against minority neighborhoods in mortgage lending (known as "redlining"), took on the same role that Aid to Families with Dependent Children (AFDC) played in the Reagan-era neoliberal imaginary. Once again, a minor program was granted the quasi-demonic power to bring the entire global economy to its knees, and this time the demonization was even more absurd, because the CRA does not even provide direct subsidies to mortgage applicants.

The Tea Party's moral discourse was also a gendered discourse, and in a much more disturbing way. Rather than focusing on any program or policy that supposedly benefited women, the first wave of Tea Party candidates was characterized by a shocking number of callous comments about rape, including claims that women could not become pregnant in cases of "legitimate rape" and that women routinely make rape accusations as a way of avoiding the embarrassment of admitting they had consensual sex with an undesirable partner.[7] These comments, which most commentators treated as bizarre non sequiturs, provoked considerable outrage, and thankfully all of the rape-apologist candidates lost their respective elections. In retrospect, however, they arguably paved the way for a presidential candidate who openly boasted on tape about committing sexual assault.

Overall, the idea that the Tea Party represented an innovative shift away from the "culture wars" quickly proved to be wishful thinking, as did the notion that Tea Partiers were primarily interested in libertarian economics and an abstractly "small" government. Like the Reagan Revolution before it—though at a considerably lower level of sophistication and refinement—the Tea Party movement represented an attempt to reassert the proper order of the household, in order to solve a moral crisis of which the economic crisis was only a symptom. The initial focus was on race and gender, but once their power was solidified in individual states, they moved on to sexual norms in the bizarre controversy over transgender bathroom access.

In contrast to the Reagan moment, however, the emphasis was not on positively cultivating desirable family structures, but on making sure that those who failed to conform were stripped of any assistance or subsidy. These efforts were pitched as an attempt to correct an injustice whereby undesirable populations had achieved unfair advantages over the more deserving straight white population. Within this outlook, blacks should not get federal housing assistance that gives them a leg up over whites, for instance, and women should not get the supposed "unfair advantage" of being able to make spurious rape accusations at will and ruin a man's reputation. This general outlook explains the seemingly ever-growing animus toward so-called political correctness, which many white men view as allowing previously subordinate populations to sit in judgment of them. The fact that these issues, rather than libertarian bromides, were the real libidinal center of gravity for the Obama-era neoconservative movement should be clear from the fact that many of those same aggrieved voters coalesced around Donald Trump, who has no apparent interest in conservative economic nostrums but virtually embodies the ideal of "political incorrectness."

My goal is not to say that we all should have seen Donald Trump coming—I certainly did not—but to point out that Trump is the culmination of a political sequence that began with the Global Financial Crisis. Nor do I intend to claim that the rise of Trump, or indeed the success of the Tea Party, was somehow predestined. In both cases they benefited from quirks in the American electoral system. Trump, of course, lost the election by millions of popular votes but took office as a result of indirect selection of the president via the Electoral College. As for the Tea Party, it maintains its stranglehold on power because of the unfortunate coincidence that its first wave election corresponded with a census year, giving it control over the redrawing of electoral district boundaries. The Tea Party took advantage of the opportunity to create gerrymandered districts that rendered it virtually impossible for Democrats to win back control of the House of Representatives even with a considerable nationwide popular-vote advantage. In both cases, of course, the Tea Party presented its manipulations and unfair advantages as necessary to counteract cheating on the other side, but such claims are almost universally rejected outside the movement itself.

Overall, then, the rise of the Tea Party and then Trump to power represented highly contingent events. The very fact that Hillary Clinton, one of the most demonized and divisive politicians in America, was able to win such a strong popular vote plurality testifies to the fact that normative neoliberalism maintains some genuine electoral legitimacy in the United States, even if only as a lesser evil. Nevertheless, the fact that such a thing was possible at all highlights one signal weakness of the neoliberal order: its ambiguous relationship to electoral democracy. Particularly in the United States, the era of normative neoliberalism witnessed declining voter participation and narrower electoral margins. Bill Clinton won only a plurality of the popular vote in both his terms; George W. Bush narrowly lost and then narrowly won the popular vote; and Hillary Clinton also won only a plurality. Only Obama achieved a clear majority for both of his terms, though by a lesser margin than Ronald Reagan or even George H. W. Bush. This situation has often been explained in terms of the political acumen of the various candidates and campaigns, but individual campaign strategies cannot account for such a durable, decades-long pattern across both major political parties.[8]

The prevalence of narrow electoral outcomes under normative neoliberalism ultimately traces back to the political-theological problem of legitimacy. A political-theological order that bases its legitimacy so overwhelmingly on individual free choice must receive the consent of the community as a whole, which happens via the electoral system. At the same time, once it is firmly established, not only does it not need a clear popular mandate for any candidate or party, but it does not desire one, because this would create unwanted expectations of large-scale change. Rather, the goal is to eke out a narrow and ambiguous victory in order to secure just enough popular legitimacy but not too much. It certainly does render the practice of electoral democracy less and less meaningful, as Brown rightly laments, but the end logic of the position is not the total abolition of democracy that Brown fears, because on the deepest level, neoliberalism relies on consent for its legitimacy.

This system produces a stable equilibrium as long as both neoliberals and neoconservatives are willing to play along and pursue broadly similar policies. Yet when an apparent challenge to the neoliberal order emerges, the tendency toward intentionally narrow victories and the reluctance to engage in serious voter mobilization creates the possibility of an upset. As seen in the case of the rape-apologist Tea Party candidates and in the case of Trump, neoliberals tend to fall back on a negative strategy of exhorting voters to reject the unacceptable opponent. This approach has often proven effective, but over the long haul, it risks exposing the mechanism of the forced choice on which neoliberal electoral politics relies. How many times can people be expected to show up and vote for the idea that this election should not even be happening in the first place, to freely endorse the prospect that there should be no alternative?

In any given case, of course, most people will accept the logic of the forced choice. Yet as we saw in our discussion of the first day of Creation, even among the very angels of the Lord, there will always be a certain number who will act out—all the more so when voting has been downgraded to an empty gesture. Many Brexit voters, for instance, reported viewing their vote as a gesture of protest, one they could afford to make because they assumed it would be impossible for Brexit to win. Surely the same logic was at work among at least some Trump voters in the three traditionally Democratic states that swung the Electoral College. If there is no alternative, if genuine change is impossible, why *not* vote as a way of letting off steam, confident that the system will prevent any seriously adverse consequences?

The curious thing about the response to both the Brexit vote—which claimed a narrow majority amid surprisingly low turnout, not the supermajority normally required for a major constitutional change—and the Trump technicality—which occurred amid suspicions of foreign interference and illegal voter suppression—is how quickly the authorities submitted to the outcomes, treating them as clear declarations of the people's will despite the ambiguities in both results. In both cases we are dealing with a huge self-inflicted wound, facilitated by authorities that clearly opposed both outcomes. The legal options were limited in the US context, but in the United Kingdom a nonbinding referendum was taken as the word of God: "Brexit means Brexit!" We can speculate about the motives of the individuals involved, but on the political-theological level, it makes a certain perverse sense. Neoliberals have always preferred the narrative of redemption, but they have not been shy about using the tools of demonization. When they find themselves repudiated, they can do nothing but take a page from the neoconservative playbook, demonizing the deplorable people who voted the wrong way and abandoning them to the suffering they have brought upon themselves. Surely by the next election they will have learned their lesson and will start making good choices again.

A Neoliberal Reaction

The unexpected success of the reactionary movement has thus given us some insight into one internal contradiction of normative neoliberalism as a political-theological paradigm: its simultaneous reliance on and minimization of popular legitimation via the electoral system. Combative neoliberalism was eager to seek out a commanding popular mandate because it needed to implement major transformative changes. By contrast, normative neoliberalism seeks a steady equilibrium in which two fundamentally similar parties pursue fundamentally similar policies. Once that dynamic breaks down, the strategies that secured neoliberal hegemony leave the system vulnerable to disruption.

With that in mind, what can we learn from the specific form that the re-action has taken? As I noted in the previous chapter, I reject the Polanyi-style analysis that claims that people are reasserting their racial and nationalist identities in the face of neoliberalism's attack on the social fabric. I have already critiqued this position from a number of angles, but here I would add that the implications of this position are both dangerous and incoherent. On the one hand, it is dangerous insofar as it naturalizes racism and nationalism as inherent features of social life, when in fact they were both constructed in the service of the very capitalist order they supposedly resist. On the other hand, it presumes a near-infinite pliability of the populations seduced by racist and nationalist solutions. Yes, they embrace the radical right now, such commentators concede, but presumably they would rush to endorse the left-wing option of expanding the welfare state if only such an option were on the table. Yet if this were the case, how could similar populations have been mobilized *against* the welfare state in the Reagan years? And how could the same anxieties and resentments have been instrumental in both the foundation and the apparent unraveling of the neoliberal order?

In reality we are not dealing with the same anxieties and resentments at all. This is because there is no sexism, homophobia, racism, nationalism, and so forth, "in general." All of these modes of oppression and exclusion take on historically specific forms and are articulated together in historically specific ways, within historically specific orders of domination. In the Reagan era, sexism, racism, and homophobia were all articulated together in response to anxieties about the consequences of the expansion of the welfare state, and the Cold War allowed for a mobilization of nationalism in simplistic good-vs.-evil terms. Since then, the situation has changed radically—most notably, the postwar welfare state has been dismantled and transformed and the "evil empire" of the Soviet Union no longer exists—and so we should expect the nature of the anxieties and resentments at play to change as well.

In the previous chapter I highlighted the ways that the neoliberal order has rearticulated white American racism against Latinos and blacks. To take the example of animus against Latinos, this newly articulated bias is in large part a response to neoliberal conditions, such as deindustrialization, declining job security, and stagnating wages. More interesting, however, is the fact that this bias has taken a distinctively neoliberal form. The general complaint is posed in explicitly economic terms—Latino immigrants are competing for jobs and driving down wages—and the conflation of all migrant workers with "illegal immigrants" implies that the success of Latino immigrants is the result of cheating ("cutting in line"). Meanwhile, little if any resentment is directed at the businesses that employ undocumented workers even though they are also breaking the law, because it is apparently taken for granted that businesses will try to cut labor costs as much as possible.

In short, the neoliberal rules of the game have been fully internalized and accepted, and the complaint is that the system is not abiding by them. A similar dynamic can be seen in all the many instances where right-wing commentators detect "unfair advantages"—cases that range from the inaccurate yet minimally plausible (affirmative action) to the incoherent (gay marriage, which is very explicitly a demand for precisely the same advantages) and the ludicrous (allowing transgender people to use the bathroom of the gender they identify with). The ideal of the "level playing field" is fully endorsed and even extended, in true neoliberal fashion, beyond the explicitly economic realm, transforming every aspect of social life into a competition.

This is not to say that the right-wing reaction is not racist. Clearly the hidden premise of their complaints is that whites are inherently more deserving and hence that in a truly level playing field, *they would win*. Since they are not winning to the degree they deserve, the game must be rigged via a whole panoply of unfair advantages handed out to their inferiors—including the "politically correct" insistence that they cannot be clearly designated as inferiors. The same can be said for the newly emergent form of nationalism. In a truly fair competition, America would always win, and if it is losing— for instance, losing manufacturing or mining jobs—that must be because of illegitimate advantages handed out to undeserving foreigners. Here there is a more overt rejection of neoliberal norms like free movement of capital or international coordination on "best practices" (above all on environmental issues), but the underlying logic is still deeply neoliberal insofar as the goal is to maximize "global competitiveness."

Hence right-wing reactionaries are not being distracted from economic interests by their indulgence in racial prejudice or nationalistic fervor, nor are they reacting against a vague feeling of social ennui or asserting a desire to be part of something bigger than themselves in an individualistic culture. They are contesting the way that specifically economic benefits are parceled out on racial and national grounds. To that extent, they are contesting the legitimacy of the neoliberal settlement, but in a partial and ambiguous way that in turn highlights an ambivalence in the neoliberal settlement itself.

What allowed for the convergence of neoconservative and neoliberal interests in the Reagan era, as we have discussed, was a shared desire to dismantle and transform the Fordist welfare state and reinforce the traditional family, along with a shared recognition that neoliberal economics would further both goals. The overlap here was so substantial that it helped to mask an important divergence: where the neoliberals wanted to reinforce traditional family structures in order to provide a foundation for their economic model, the neoconservatives wanted to create a neoliberal economic model in order to reinforce traditional family structures. This difference in emphasis is potentially a much more serious problem on the political-theological level insofar as it calls into question the ultimate root of the system's legitimacy: is it the family structure or the economic model? Which is means and which is end?

As outgrowths of the neoconservative wing of the neoliberal settlement, the Tea Party and Trump question the legitimacy of the system on the basis of its outcomes: white patriarchal families, in their view, are unfairly falling behind in relation to undesirable and undeserving populations. Yet after a generation in which neoconservatism and neoliberalism have been so deeply intertwined, it seems unimaginable that the neoliberal economic model could be fundamentally illegitimate. There is an underlying faith that the free market, if properly structured, would still deliver the "correct" outcomes. We can see this, first of all, in the lack of any serious consideration of any direct government action to shore up white patriarchal families, such as a job guarantee or government subsidies. Even Trump's plan to repair crumbling infrastructure—a relatively noncontroversial target for direct state investment—amounts to a complex public-private partnership in the grand neoliberal style, relying on tax credits and promises of privatization to nudge private firms to take part in renewing the nation's roads and bridges.[9] And more broadly, much of the focus has been on traditional libertarian themes such as tax cuts and deregulation rather than any positive economic intervention on the part of the state. Belief in the providential hand of the market appears to be unshaken.

It is also noteworthy that there appears to be no effort to positively enhance the life-chances of white patriarchal families (through investment in
education and job training, for instance), nor is there the kind of exhortation
to moral uprightness that is often directed at black fathers. Instead, the emphasis is on all the ways the most deserving populations have been cheated:
the unfair advantages given to other groups, the bad trade deals that favor
foreign countries over America, the global conspiracy to discredit the fossil
fuels that power the American dream. As the last example shows, this line
of thinking can quickly head in paranoid directions, but if we focus on the
factual untruth of the claim, we risk missing its emotional root—namely, the
conviction that good, hardworking Americans have been lied to.

In the previous chapter I cited the principle of "*Volenti non fit injuria*"—to
the willing person no wrong can be done—which Cooper summarizes as
"the legal translation of the idea that risk, once consented to, must be borne
entirely by the individual, unless one can prove fraud or duress in the performance of a contract."[10] Neoconservatives have traditionally deployed this
principle against disadvantaged populations as a means of victim-blaming.
The paranoid grievances of the Tea Party and Trump draw on that same
principle to paint themselves as victims—of liberal elites who sold out their
country, of systems rigged in favor of minorities, of an illegitimate president
who faked his birth certificate. The competition *must* be fraudulent, because
the only alternative is to face the unbearable shame of admitting that they
competed and lost, fair and square.

Hence the very deepest neoliberal presuppositions—above all, the ones
that affect us at the most profound emotional level—remain very much in
place. This is not to say that the Tea Party and Trump simply "are" neoliberal,
but to emphasize that the contemporary reaction is very much a reaction
to neoliberalism, and one that is certainly not ready to abandon neoliberalism altogether. In theological terms it represents not an apostasy, not a
total renunciation of the neoliberal faith, but a heresy. Here we should avoid
misunderstanding: though there is a tendency to valorize heretics as reb-
els against Christianity, heresies can be better understood as an attempt to
reclaim and purify Christianity. Despite the negative results that they perceive in mainstream institutional Christianity, heretics want very much
to believe that Christianity is good and desirable, and they will construct

whatever narrative allows them to preserve that belief. Thus from a contemporary perspective, many heresies—including Luther's Protestantism, which was regarded as a heresy by the Catholic authorities of the time—amount to paranoid conspiracy theories about the illegitimate authorities that have hijacked and corrupted the gospel.[11] In the same way, our present-day neoliberal heretics want to believe that the providential hand of the market rewards the deserving, and they want to believe that they are among the deserving (conceived in the explicitly neoliberal terms of winning the economic competition). And if reality does not match up with those beliefs, then so much the worse for reality.

I Want to Believe

It is here that we enter into the realm of "fake news" and "alternative facts"—two terms that have themselves ironically been caught up in a conspiracy theory about Russian interference in the 2016 election.[12] This is not to say that Russian hackers did not in fact plant false news stories, leak damaging information, and attempt to infiltrate voting machines.[13] As far as I am able to discern, those events really did happen. Yet those true facts have been taken up into a narrative that has the structure of a conspiracy theory, which personalizes and externalizes events and outcomes that really result from impersonal systemic forces. The classic conspiracy theory is of course anti-Semitism, which blames a conspiracy of Jewish leaders for the depredations of the capitalist system. It can't be the case that our economic system has been intentionally structured in a way that produces these harmful outcomes, the anti-Semite reasons, and so it must be the result of scheming foreigners. Similarly, from the liberal-progressive perspective, it can't be the case that a substantial plurality of their fellow citizens were willing to choose Trump over the most qualified candidate in American history, so the painful election result must stem from enemy interference.

Conspiracy theories are often associated with traumatic events such as the Kennedy assassination or 9/11. In contrast to paranoid anti-Semitism, however, the conspiracy theories associated with those events display the reverse logic: an event that really was contingent and exogenous is explained as an internal conspiracy among elites. It cannot be the case that some Marxist oddball could be in a position to kill the president nor that a bunch of guys with box cutters could hijack planes and kill thousands. Such events would call the strength and security of the United States into question, rendering the world's great superpower a passive victim of chance events. The conspiracy theory restores American omnipotence, even if in an evil form. As Jodi Dean puts it with reference to 9/11 "Truther" conspiracies: "Countering the official story of passivity, here the government acts, ruthlessly. It's organized, efficient, able to execute its plans without a hitch."[14] Some versions of the liberal conspiracy theory echo this structure, most notably the view that then-FBI Director James Comey's late-breaking revelation of an additional cache of Clinton emails represented intentional interference in the election. This leads to the strange belief that the very same Deep State that (in the person of Comey) threw the election to Trump could just as easily reverse the result (again in the person of Comey, this time imagined as the hero whose congressional testimony will lead to Trump's impeachment). Comey can't simply be a career bureaucrat who made some questionable decisions about how to handle a politically awkward situation. He must be a villain or a hero—either one will do.

Such patterns of thinking are of course much more widespread, and much less fact-based, on the political right. Especially when they concern Hillary Clinton, conspiracy theories can take on lurid and disturbing forms, such as the claim—whose proponents include Michael Flynn, who served briefly as Trump's national security advisor—that the former First Lady and secretary of state was running a child-molestation ring out of a pizza parlor.[15] This theory, dubbed "Pizzagate," epitomizes the trend of "fake news" that was quickly seized upon as an explanation for Trump's Electoral College upset (and put forward as the primary mechanism by which the Russians intervened in the election). Surely, from the neoliberal perspective, people cannot have objectively assessed Hillary Clinton and Donald Trump and decided that Trump was preferable, at least not in sufficient numbers to hand him the presidency. That would call into question all the deepest neoliberal convictions about meritocracy and the value of expertise. The problem must be that they were lied to and misled. And for good measure, these lies must have come from a foreign source.

It should be clear by now that we are not dealing primarily with an epistemological problem here. "Fake news" stories, like conspiracy theories in general, must be understood as a political-theological phenomenon. They represent last-ditch efforts to save an order of legitimacy and meaning that is breaking down—a state of affairs that the conspiratorial narrative both denies and unconsciously acknowledges. On the one hand, the conspiracy theories will go to any length to save the horizon of meaning that they perceive as threatened, even to the point of embracing absurdities (single mothers on welfare have the power to destroy American society) or outright contradictions (the only hope for democracy is a coup by the state security apparatus). On the other hand, the immanence of collapse is inscribed into the narratives themselves, which often take on an apocalyptic form: it is always the *last chance* to save freedom or democracy or truth or America or the traditional family in the final battle against an enemy that is simultaneously strong enough to win permanently and yet weak enough to be utterly defeated.[16]

Neoliberalism has always had an apocalyptic edge. This is clear enough in its initial combative stage, when it freely deployed the rhetoric of demonization and evoked a world-historical struggle against evil. One might be tempted to dismiss this as a result of the necessary alliance with social conservatives and hence as extrinsic to neoliberalism proper, yet already in its prehistory as an intellectual movement far from the centers of power, neoliberal ideology could take on an apocalyptic tone. Friedrich Hayek's *Road to Serfdom*, published in the same year as Polanyi's *The Great Transformation* (1944), argues that the embrace of the welfare state and economic planning will lead Western countries inexorably toward a Soviet-style command economy, completely destroying market freedoms and hence freedom as such.[17] This theory is paranoid in its structure, using the logic of guilt-by-association to turn diametrically opposed political ideologies—most notably Fascism and Communism—into so many faces of a global conspiracy against freedom, which only the faithful remnant of economic liberals are brave enough to expose for what it is.

Once the evil empire of central planning was defeated and its domestic counterpart transformed beyond recognition, it could appear that apocalyptic rhetoric was no longer called for. At first glance, the transition seems straightforward: where the neoliberals of the combative era could view themselves as God's army, defeating the demonic forces of Communism and the welfare state, the neoliberal order of the normative era was the Kingdom of Heaven itself, the hard-won Promised Land that comes after the titanic struggle against the enemies of freedom. Yet the situation is more complex than that, because the threat of apocalypse still loomed in the form of resurgent nationalism, extremism, terrorism, and other symptoms of irrational rebellion against the neoliberal order. The duty of the normative neoliberal was to keep such forces at bay, to restrain them. In other words, apocalypse is still very much in play, but it has taken on a different valence: it means not victory but defeat, not hope but disaster.

The combative neoliberal stance represents a more familiar and straight-forward apocalyptic narrative, where the self-identified righteous ones long for the final battle with the forces of evil, in which God will win once and for all and his followers will be vindicated. The early Christian movement held to a version of this narrative. Though it incorporated the seemingly counter-intuitive detail that the death of the messiah at the hands of the demonic imperial authorities was actually a necessary first step in the apocalyptic sequence, early believers still hoped for God's ultimate victory, which many of them expected to occur within their own lifetime. As the final consummation was deferred—and, perhaps more importantly, as Christianity unexpectedly found itself no longer a persecuted sect but rather the official religion of the once-hated empire—attitudes shifted. As in the shift between combative and normative neoliberalism, the thought of apocalypse became a site of anxiety rather than triumph.

Emblematic here are two short books of the New Testament, the First and Second Letters to the Thessalonians.[18] The first letter, potentially the very earliest of all Christian writings, was composed by Paul the Apostle to comfort a community of Christ-followers he had founded. Some members of the group had died, leading the others to worry that their fallen comrades might miss out on the new world God was soon to inaugurate. Paul reassures them that no one will be left out:

> For since we believe that Jesus died and rose again, even so, through Jesus, God will bring with him those who have died. For this we declare to you by the word of the Lord, that we who are alive, who are left until the coming of the Lord, will by no means precede those who have died. For the Lord

himself, with a cry of command, with the archangel's call and with the sound of God's trumpet, will descend from heaven, and the dead in Christ will rise first. Then we who are alive, who are left, will be caught up in the clouds together with them to meet the Lord in the air; and so we will be with the Lord forever. Therefore encourage one another with these words. (1 Thessalonians 4:14–18)

The promise is one of total restoration, in which even death itself will be overcome and all believers will enjoy the fullness of God's presence for all eternity. It is something to look forward to—and, as indicated by the use of the present tense ("we who *are* alive"), it is something that will happen while Paul and at least some of his recipients are still alive. By contrast, the Second Letter to the Thessalonians, which also claims to come from Paul but which many scholars now believe was actually a later author's attempt to "correct" Paul's apocalyptic claims,[19] paints a more frightening picture:

Let no one deceive you in any way; for that day [of Judgment] will not come unless the rebellion comes first and the lawless one is revealed, the one destined for destruction. He opposes and exalts himself above every so-called god or object of worship, so that he takes his seat in the temple of God, declaring himself to be God. Do you not remember that I told you these things when I was still with you? And you know what is now restraining him, so that he may be revealed when his time comes. For the mystery of lawlessness is already at work, but only until the one who now restrains it is removed. And then the lawless one will be revealed, whom the Lord Jesus will destroy with the breath of his mouth, annihilating him by the manifestation of his coming. (2 Thessalonians 2:3–8)

Here there is virtually none of the apocalyptic hope we saw in First Thessalonians. Instead the author focuses almost exclusively on the destruction that will be wrought by the "man of lawlessness" once the force or individual restraining him is removed. God is still going to win out in the end, but perhaps the restrainer is a better bet for the time being.

The figure of the restrainer (usually designated with the Greek term *katechon*) has been the object of considerable reflection in the field of political theology. Carl Schmitt has argued that the *katechon* was the central concept of Christian politics, allowing it to bracket its apocalyptic expectations and get to work creating political institutions in this present world,[20] and many thinkers have argued that the concept of the modern state is a secularized version of this figure who restrains the forces of apocalyptic destruction.[21] We can certainly hear an echo of this logic in Polanyi's view of the state as a necessary counterweight to the demonic forces of the unrestrained market—a polarity that the neoliberal opponents of the Fordist social welfare state would in turn reverse.

Once neoliberalism gains global hegemony in the normative era, market forces and technocratic expertise are presented as a means to restrain the destructive forces of political conflict by channeling humanity's competitive instincts into the mutually beneficial pursuit of economic prosperity. This gesture prompts Brown's apocalyptic narrative in which the window for saving the space of political contestation is rapidly closing and we risk losing authentic freedom for good. I have already argued that this concern is exaggerated insofar as neoliberalism needs electoral legitimation and its electoral strategy is inherently vulnerable to upsets like the Trump technicality. Even if Trump himself was far from inevitable, some comparable fluke was bound to happen eventually.

Here I want to take a step further: the neoliberal attempt at depoliticization directly generates the right-wing reaction that it is meant to restrain. The very gesture of presenting ostensibly "neutral" categories like expertise, merit, evidence, and so forth as the grounds of legitimacy for the neoliberal order politicizes them. Neoliberals in the age of "alternative facts" bemoan the loss of any factual point of reference that can carry authority for all political actors, but this neutrality was a casualty of neoliberalism itself. Instead of being a neutral arbiter between political opponents, knowledge was identified with one side in a political struggle.

Within each major party in the United States, the neoliberal "centrist" position represented reason and realism, while those who would contest the neoliberal consensus supposedly traded in irrationality and fantasy. Meanwhile, when it came time for the general election, both parties initially vied to be seen as the avatar of authentic knowledge—although this fragile dynamic had already begun to break down in the 2000 US election, which pitted the cerebral Al Gore against the incurious George W. Bush. And we would do well to remember in this context that the Bush years saw the first emergence of "fake news," in the form of satirical news outlets like *The Daily Show*. An atmosphere of cynical knowingness pervades the liberal version of "fake news," which ridicules Republicans as liars and fools. This ridicule is mostly deserved, but the concrete function of liberal "fake news" is to further the politicization of knowledge through the implicit claim that intelligence and honesty are the sole prerogative of centrist (neo)liberals.

Such a dynamic is especially pernicious when we recognize the increasingly high economic stakes of knowledge and expertise in the normative neoliberal era. Higher education is presented as virtually the sole path, not only to class mobility, but even to maintaining a middle-class lifestyle across generations. At the same time, the neoliberal era has witnessed a precipitous decline in public support for higher education, which is no longer conceived as a public good but as an attempt at increasing one's individual income and career opportunities. Cooper documents how increased reliance on student loans, which began as a convenient legislative compromise between Reagan and Democrats in Congress, was "reformulated as a deliberate component of social policy" under Clinton, opening up more economic opportunities for the disadvantaged.[22] As Brown bemoans, saddling students with student loans is a highly effective means of forcing them to think about their education in solely economic terms as an investment.[23] This mind-set leads, as Morgan Adamson points out, to the view that education is "a capital investment aimed at building equity over time, much like an investment in real estate or financial stock."[24] This instrumentalization of education and expertise further contributes to the decline of any shared point of reference for assessing political or even factual claims (as in climate change denialism).

When we confront the contemporary "fake news" phenomenon, then, we are not dealing solely with the stupidity or stubbornness of individuals, but with a dynamic generated by neoliberalism itself. Conspiracy theories about how mainstream politicians and media outlets manipulate facts to serve their own power are often disturbingly wrong on the level of content, but they are true on the level of form. The neoliberal order really does instrumentalize knowledge to secure economic advantage and political legitimacy. What has changed in recent years is that the neoliberal claim to have privileged access to reality has been shattered in the era of punitive neoliberalism, not only by the Global Financial Crisis, but arguably even more by the mass suffering caused by dogmatic adherence to the neoliberal model in the aftermath. The supposed experts not only failed to predict and prevent the crisis, but they lacked the ability to clean up the mess afterward.

Hence we can begin to understand the paradoxical poll results showing that many people found Donald Trump more trustworthy than Hillary Clinton. In his obviously self-serving lies, Trump appeared more "honest" on a deeper level than Clinton, because he seemed to present the same face in every context. By contrast, Clinton's calculated reserve—arguably even more than her secret Wall Street speeches or the hacking of her emails—opened up a space for speculation about her "real" motives, which could be assumed to be sinister from the very fact that she was hiding them. Clinton is of course a special case, because she has virtually embodied neoconservative anxieties about gender relations since she came on the political scene in her husband's campaign and hence has been the subject of a harsh demonization campaign for decades. Yet in the postcrisis era, arguably any neoliberal candidate would be subject to the same charges of two-faced dishonesty, precisely because of their polish and sophistication. And all of this is predictable blowback of the neoliberal strategy to claim knowledge and expertise as the foundation of political legitimacy—in other words, the restrainer created the very force it has now so spectacularly failed to restrain.

Foreclosing the Future

One of the most alarming political developments of the Obama years was Republican intransigence on raising the federal debt ceiling. Originally created to save Congress the trouble of approving each individual decision to issue Treasury bonds, the ceiling allows the government to use debt funding up to a certain level, which up until the Tea Party revolution was periodically raised as a matter of course. Threatening to disrupt this routine was exceptionally reckless and dangerous. If Congress had really refused to increase the debt ceiling, it would have led to a default on the US national debt, triggering a second—and potentially much more severe—financial crisis within only a few years.

It would be a mistake to view the debt ceiling crisis as simply another case of political brinkmanship, however. In reality it was a crisis of legitimacy. Mainstream commentators implicitly recognized this when they decried the Republicans' reckless endangerment of the "full faith and credit of the United States," with some suggesting that willfully triggering a default may even be unconstitutional, owing to a post–Civil War amendment forbidding the repudiation of government debt. For their part, Republicans more or less openly questioned the legitimacy of the national debt as such, which they consistently associated with the social programs that they revile. After a generation of neoliberal policy, of course, social spending was an even more trivial part of the federal budget than the programs demonized in the Reagan era, and in general there was no reason to believe that the national debt—which has steadily increased over the more than two centuries of US history—had reached some kind of threshold that would render it suddenly unsustainable on an economic level.

Lacking any factual basis for an apocalyptic debt scare, then, the Tea Party created its own. And in this, Tea Partiers were exceptional only in their hardball tactics—as Davies points out, the era of "punitive neoliberalism" saw a wave of brutal austerity measures that were legitimated by the need to rein in government debt. As discussed above, such policies were actually counterproductive even on their own terms, as reduced government employment and spending produced a drag on economic growth that more than outweighed the cost savings achieved through austerity. Here, as Davies suggests, punitive neoliberalism shows itself to be governed not by cold economic calculation but by a depraved moral calculus: "Under punitive neoliberalism, economic dependency and moral failure become entangled in the form of debt, producing a melancholic condition in which governments and societies unleash hatred and violence upon members of their own populations. When debt is combined with political weakness, it becomes a condition for further punishment" (130). The optimistic tone of normative neoliberalism gives way to sheer sadism and victim blaming. As my political-theological analysis has shown, however, this is not a break with neoliberalism but a fulfillment of its deepest logic, insofar as neoliberalism is an order based on the moral entrapment that I have called demonization.

Neoliberalism's increasing reliance on debt represents an attempt to moralize or, as Brown puts it, "responsibilize" ever more areas of life. The increasing burden of officially quantified debt represents a strategy to render one's moral obligations more easily and precisely extractable.[25] From this perspective the fact that student debt is one of the only forms of debt not dischargeable through bankruptcy in the United States makes perfect sense: the human capital the student has accumulated (or more precisely, had the opportunity to accumulate, since a growing number of student loan debtors never complete their degrees) is inalienable. Unlike in the case of a mortgage loan, where the lender gains title to the house if the borrower defaults, there is no possibility of foreclosing on the human capital (or failure to accumulate human capital) that is intrinsic to one's own person. If the borrowers do not get the full benefit of that human capital in the form of the promised higher income, so the reasoning goes, that is their own fault, and their personal failure does not cancel their obligation to make good on the lender's investment. Indeed, it only intensifies that debt, as penalties, fees, and skyrocketing interest rates can leave student loan borrowers with staggering balances that dwarf the original loan disbursements. Yet even if literal foreclosure is not possible in such cases, the nondischargeability of student loan debt does represent a figurative foreclosure of the borrower's future as such. An open future, filled with a range of opportunities and options, is transmuted into a virtual enslavement to an unpayable debt.

As we have seen, the earliest stages of capitalism and the classical era of Polanyi's "one-hundred years' peace" both relied on geographic colonization. In a world where there is increasingly no outside to colonize, no significant territory that has yet to be incorporated into the capitalist order, we can view the explosion of debt as a form of temporal colonization, using the future itself as a site of primitive accumulation. This temporal colonization, like its geographical counterpart, does not produce simple uniformity. Just as uneven geographical development serves a productive purpose in the capitalist system, so too can variations in life chances be converted into varying levels of "risk" to be incorporated into complex financial strategies—in subprime loans, for instance, which actually prove more profitable, not despite but because of the fact that they are less likely to be paid off.

Overall, though, neoliberal financialization is an attempt to tame the future through the use of legal instruments that mandate the reproduction of the present. As Lazzarato points out, debt achieves this not solely through creating enforceable obligations but by shaping human subjectivity itself:

"Debt is not only an economic mechanism, it is also a security-state technique of government aimed at reducing the uncertainty of the behavior of the governed. By training the governed to 'promise' (to honor their debt), capitalism exercises 'control over the future,' since debt obligations allow one to foresee, calculate, measure, and establish equivalences between current and future behavior. The effects of the power of debt on subjectivity (guilt and responsibility) allow capitalism to bridge the gap between present and future."[26] Here again, student loans are exemplary, because they force students to think of their educational choices in financial terms and of themselves as customers. This effect extends far beyond their graduation date, as public service and artistic pursuits appear much less realistic than corporate jobs in light of their high debt load—meaning that the capitalist class gets the direct benefit of the "human capital" that the student has paid the up-front cost of creating, along with the interest payments. And this is the most generous version of the dynamic, which in the case of predatory payday lenders takes the brutal and direct form of reproducing present poverty by extracting ever-increasing portions of the debtor's income.

Yet this drive to settle accounts with the future, to perpetually "preempt" it,[27] to restrain its apocalyptic implications, runs up against the stubborn obstacle that unaccountable events continue to happen. This renders the neoliberal order exceptionally fragile, not merely on an economic or political level but on the level of legitimacy. Its spurious claim to have accounted for the future in advance, its ruthless exploitation of the future as a means of propping up the present, means that the only thing that can *happen*, the only possible *event* in the strong sense, is a catastrophe.[28]

With this in mind we can understand why the neoliberal end of history is an era marked by crisis and terrorism. Terrorism is presented as the unforeseeable eruption of violence from the outside, from those who refuse the neoliberal order of freedom and rationality, while crisis represents an endogenous but still unforeseen threat. Familiar strategies of nationalism and scapegoating mean that terrorism, far from challenging the legitimacy of the neoliberal order, has actually reinforced it. Yet the situation is different in the case of crises, which cannot be as easily blamed on outsiders and which tend to expose the weakness and ineptitude of the governing authorities. The Global Financial Crisis is a case in point: the complex financial instruments that triggered the crisis were based on the assumption that a simultaneous nationwide real-estate downturn was impossible, yet the demand for the offending securities actually created the conditions for the supposedly impossible possibility by generating an unprecedented simultaneous nationwide real-estate bubble.[29] Neither the supposed financial visionaries who created the scheme nor the government officials responsible for regulating them could anticipate such consequences, however, so deeply engrained was the assumption that the future would be fundamentally like the present.[30]

Here we can see the insidious contradiction in the normative neoliberal attempt to replace social benefits with access to credit. On the political-economic level, Cooper is right to voice skepticism: "How, after all, is it possible to overcome inequality by democratizing a legal instrument that is intended by its very nature to privatize wealth? Is social democracy achievable through the generalization of inheritance?"[31] Yet the problem is deeper: how can we increase people's freedom and independence by democratizing a legal instrument that is intended to create obligation and servitude? How can we open up people's future by democratizing a legal instrument that channels all future possibilities into revenue streams? How long can a society endure if it can experience the unexpected only as violence and catastrophe, never as surprise and creativity? How long can people tolerate living in a society where every opportunity and promise is convertible into a threat and a trap?

In the face of the right-wing doubling-down on neoliberalism, we might be tempted to answer: "Surprisingly long!" Yet even in their grotesque parody of neoliberalism at its worst, one can detect a countervailing demand for neoliberalism to finally end. In the refusal to raise the debt ceiling, for instance, one could hear a refusal of a culture structured around debt, and more fundamentally, in the demand for the "right" people to permanently win the competition, one can discern a desire to escape from competition once and for all. Even in the people who seem to demand neoliberalism the most, then, there is a strong undercurrent of discontent, albeit one that has so far manifested itself only in the unedifying spectacle of politicians victimizing others while perpetually claiming to be the real victims.

More promising is the discontent of the younger generation, which has driven the unexpected success of politicians like Bernie Sanders and Jeremy Corbyn. Where Wendy Brown envisions future generations of neoliberal drones who have forgotten how to want political change, our contemporary experience shows that it is precisely the generation that has known nothing but neoliberalism that is most likely to reject it. The order that strove to shape the entire world in its image—nay, to reshape human nature itself!— appears to be failing spectacularly in the core task of any political-theological paradigm: ensuring that it is accepted and reproduced by the next generation.

If our present political moment teaches us anything, then, it teaches us that neoliberalism is not sustainable. This is not because it is economically inefficient (though it is), nor is it because it embraces an inherently fragile political strategy (though it does). The root problem is at the level of political theology: its approach to self-legitimation is self-undermining. The very strategies that it uses to justify itself and its outcomes inevitably create subjects who are anxious, ashamed, resentful, and exhausted. It may well hold out through inertia or through presenting itself as a lesser evil compared to the right-wing reaction, or it may attempt to convert itself into a more overtly coercive order. But neoliberalism will never again appear as the righteous insurgent of the combative period or as the self-evident order of the normative period.

The spell has been broken—or rather, it has collapsed, and therein lies the difficulty. Neoliberalism has lost its aura of inevitability, but at the same time no comprehensive alternative has presented itself. Though I cannot pretend to know in detail what that alternative will look like if and when it arises, in the time that remains I will attempt to sketch out some indications of how we might recognize it when it comes.

AFTER NEOLIBERALISM

My goal in this book has been not only to offer an analysis of neoliberalism, but to think through the ways that political theology would have to change in order to be equal to the task of such an analysis. While conceding that neoliberalism would not count as a paradigm of political theology in strict Schmittian terms, I argued in the first chapter that we can see in Schmitt's own work a broader vision of political theology, of which the standard Schmittian model would be only a narrow subset. This general theory of political theology would be defined not by particular classic themes—such as the homology between divine and human sovereignty and the problem of the transition from medieval Christianity to secular modernity—but as an inquiry into the ways that human communities try to justify their structures of governance (the political problem of legitimacy) and make sense of their experience of suffering and injustice (the theological problem of evil).

With this expanded notion of political theology in mind, I went on to challenge the conventional understanding of its constituent terms. In my second chapter I argued that the "political" in political theology cannot be understood in terms of "Arendt's axiom," according to which there is (or at least should be) an absolute qualitative distinction between the political and the economic. And in the following chapter I made the case that the most salient theological theme for understanding neoliberalism is not divine sovereignty but creaturely free will—reflecting my view that the "theology" in political theology cannot be understood solely as a discourse about God. Finally, I characterized neoliberalism's strategy of self-legitimation as an apocalyptic one and interpreted the contemporary right-wing reaction as a heretical variation on neoliberalism rather than a comprehensive break with it, insofar as the right-wing reaction still embraces the neoliberal conception of the sources of legitimacy.

Now, as I turn to the question of what might make for a genuine alternative to neoliberalism, my first step will be to consolidate my general theory of political theology by way of a definition: *Political theology is a holistic, genealogical inquiry into the structures and sources of legitimacy in a particular historical moment.* Political theology in this sense is *political* because it investigates institutions and practices of governance (whether they are defined as state-based or economic, public or private), and it is *theological* because it deals with questions of meaning and value (regardless of the form the answers take). And it is both *simultaneously* because the structures of governance are always necessarily caught up with questions of meaning and value and because the answers we offer to questions of meaning and value always have direct implications for how the world should be governed—in other words, the *structures and sources of legitimacy* tend to correlate conceptually. It is *holistic* in the sense that it tends toward a total account of the structures of legitimacy, both institutional and discursive, in a given time and place, and it is *genealogical* in that it sees those structures not as static givens or abstract doctrines, but as a result of strategy and struggle. That it is both at once means that its holism does not lead to something like a "systematic political theology" but instead serves as a heuristic device for uncovering sites of breakdown and contradiction within any given political theological paradigm. And it is assured of finding such sites because every political theological paradigm represents a contingent strategic outcome within *a particular historical moment*—never a universal or final answer, because both the problem of legitimacy and the problem of evil are ultimately insoluble.

That political theology seeks after sites of breakdown and contradiction does not mean that it is always on the lookout for superficial hypocrisy, such as a difference between ideological proclamations and concrete practice. Take, for example, the frequent observation among critics of neoliberalism that neoliberals *say* they want to let the free market work, but *actually* they rely on the state—an accusation that appears to be well-nigh irresistible, even for critics who are well aware of the central role of the state in constructing the neoliberal order. This attack is highly suspect from a political theological perspective because it takes for granted the neoliberal distinction between state and market.

Against such an acceptance of the neoliberal terms of debate, I have argued from the beginning that one of the distinctive traits of political theology is its refusal of seemingly commonsense binaries. This commitment is announced in its very name, which breaks down secular modernity's division between the political and the religious, and I argued in the second chapter that it should be just as critical of the dyad of the political and the economic. One benefit of this broad vision of political theology is that it would allow for a broader view of the core texts of the discipline. Indeed, one of the most curious aspects of political theology as presently understood is that Weber's *Protestant Ethic and the Spirit of Capitalism* is not considered a foundational document alongside Schmitt's and Kantorowicz's work.[1] What ultimately motivates this breaking down of the political-economic binary, however, is not simply a desire to expand the purview of political theology, but rather a recognition that political theological paradigms legitimate themselves precisely by means of the core conceptual distinctions they set up.

In the case of neoliberalism, the distinction between state and market—which has functioned in different ways at different moments in the history of modern capitalism—is articulated in such a way as to reinforce neoliberal hegemony by forestalling the emergence of power centers guided by non-neoliberal priorities. Libertarian clichés play into this process by simultaneously naturalizing the market and painting the state as an incompetent blunderer at best and a prototalitarian oppressor at worst. Within this framework, any autonomous action on the part of the state, uninformed by the economic imperatives formulated by neoliberal technocrats, is illegitimate. And the irresistible hypocrisy attack ironically echoes this logic, insofar as it presents state action as something shameful that must be hidden.

Political theology cannot accept any static, normative distinction between the political and the economic because it recognizes that every political theological paradigm represents a transformation and redistribution of authoritative categories. This means that political theology is always necessarily concerned with change, because each order arises out of the ruins of its predecessors and each order is threatened with dissolution in its turn. We cannot understand neoliberalism except in the context of the decline in Fordism, just as we cannot understand Fordism apart from the world-historical crises that arose from the breakdown of the "hundred years' peace" of classical liberalism. At the same time, political theology is not a teleological discipline. Political theological paradigms do not emerge from some inner necessity of the historical process but through conflict and creativity.

In our specific context, this means that neoliberalism was not the only possible response to the crisis of Fordism in the early 1970s. As Melinda Cooper reminds us, there were many possibilities in play at that historical moment, many of which seem almost inconceivably radical from our present perspective. The victory of neoliberalism was a contingent outcome that depended in part on the skillful manipulation of the resentments and anxieties that arose out of the contradictions within the Fordist paradigm. Things really could have turned out differently, and we would be living in a very different world if they had—possibly even a world in which neoliberal policy prescriptions, far from being the only "realistic" option, would appear laughably foolish.

This is not to say that political theology represents a sheer voluntarism, but its emphasis on human agency makes it a valuable counterweight to the determinism and claustrophobia that often characterize the Marxist and Foucauldian approaches that have so far dominated the analysis of neoliberalism. To paraphrase Marx, political theology in the broadest sense teaches that human beings create their structures of meaning and legitimacy, but not in conditions of their own choosing. This emphasis on contingency and human agency is particularly important to keep in mind in our present moment, when so many commentators, both mainstream and academic, are tempted to declare the right-wing reaction to be the inevitable outcome of neoliberalism.

As I tried to show in the previous chapter, the right-wing reaction is indeed legible as one *possible* outcome of the neoliberal frame, one that pushes certain core convictions to their logical extreme. Yet from a political theological perspective, it is neither a genuine alternative to neoliberalism nor a particularly robust variation on the theme. For political theology as for classical democratic theory, political power relies on the consent of the governed—no structure of legitimacy and meaning can long survive if the people it is supposed to govern do not believe in it. As Bonnie Honig points out, even Carl Schmitt's "neo-Hobbesian" political theory "has democratic qualities: It postulates popular subscription to sovereign power."[2] And in contrast to both combative and normative neoliberalism, punitive neoliberalism and the right-wing reaction that evolves out of it are profoundly lacking in popular support and seem to have no interest in democratic legitimacy.

The right-wing reactionaries may yet be able to cling to power through institutional quirks or outright violence. They will do great damage if they succeed in doing so, at great human cost. Yet we must never lose sight of the fact that they are, on the most fundamental level, *weak*. Even leaving aside the implausibility of their political agenda, which is based on a heady mixture of magical thinking and conspiracy theories, their lack of popular legitimacy means that they simply do not represent a viable long-term alternative to the neoliberal paradigm. In fact, as demonstrated by the outcome of the recent French election, they may have given neoliberalism a new lease on life, with the shambles of Trump and Brexit serving as cautionary tales. If there is to be a right-wing alternative to neoliberalism, it will have to take a very different form, led by very different people.

Prospects for a Return to Fordism

The same two countries that have provided the most vivid illustrations of the right-wing reaction have also witnessed the emergence of two leaders who promise to break with the neoliberal consensus from the left: Bernie Sanders in the United States and Jeremy Corbyn in the United Kingdom. Though neither has taken power at the time of this writing, both are enjoying surging popularity—particularly among the younger generation—in an environment where their neoliberal centrist colleagues seem utterly incapable of capturing the public imagination. Both are veterans of the political struggles of the 1960s, and hence they represent a kind of pre-neoliberal remnant within their respective parties (treating Sanders as a de facto Democrat despite his official status as an Independent). Both are witnesses to an era when any number of policies that are dubbed impossible today (more generous welfare and health provision, for example, or fully state-funded higher education) were living realities, and though their movements have also attracted more radical elements, both Sanders and Corbyn are essentially promising a return to some version of the Fordist welfare state.

Such an outcome would be far preferable, in my view, to either the normative neoliberal status quo ante or the right-wing reaction's cruel parody of punitive neoliberalism. And I would postulate that such an outcome is possible in principle: the material resources necessary to achieve it clearly exist, and although the political obstacles are considerable, it would be shortsighted to assume that political conditions cannot change, especially at a time when we are witnessing so many unexpected events. That being said, however, here as in the previous chapter, I do not aspire to prognostication or punditry. My task is to assess the prospects for a return to Fordism on the level of political theology. What are its prospects for effecting the profound conceptual and moral changes needed to create a genuine new paradigm to replace neoliberalism? More than that, can we reasonably expect a renewed Fordism to represent a robust and durable alternative to neoliberalism?

On both fronts there are grounds for ambivalence, if not pessimism. First and foremost, the original Fordist settlement arose under vastly different circumstances. All the major Western countries had mobilized for total war, and most had witnessed untold destruction. In the latter countries it made sense for the state to take the lead in repairing the damage, while in the United States, which had escaped virtually unscathed, the shift from the Second World War to the Cold War meant that the state maintained a heavy hand in economic development for military reasons. These circumstances contributed to the legitimacy of the Fordist paradigm, as private industry and the general public not only accepted but expected state support and leadership on economic matters.

Both material conditions and the political consensus are radically different today. For a generation and more, state institutions have essentially "outsourced" industrial policy to the financial sector and the neoliberal technocrats who serve their priorities. A more assertive, autonomous role for the state in directing investment and development has become unthinkable. Even in the emergency circumstances of the Global Financial Crisis, direct state ownership or management of financial firms—where state and capital have been most tightly intertwined throughout the neoliberal era—was never seriously considered as an option. The bailouts of the US auto industry featured a larger role for the state in brokering the deal, but here again, the goal was to get things "back to normal," not to assert a greater independent role for the state in guiding industry, much less owning and operating firms.

Similarly, the experience of wartime rationing and mass conscription in the United States made it much easier to justify an aggressive tax policy and great generosity to the working and middle classes—after all, they had sacrificed a great deal. Meanwhile, greater controls over capital movement and a broad consensus in favor of higher taxes among developed nations made it harder for the wealthy to flee taxation. Neoliberalism has broken down the kind of social solidarity enjoyed in the immediate postwar era, and now countries compete to lower their tax rates to attract wealthy investors. Recognition of this latter challenge has led many proponents of a return to Fordism to find unexpected common ground with the right-wing reaction in proposing trade restrictions, with Sanders going so far as to say that he would happily work with Trump on that issue.[3] Yet the act of restricting foreign imports will not in itself cause domestic replacements to arise and could hurt existing domestic producers who rely on global supply chains. Free trade promised that cheap consumer goods would make up for American losses in wages and job security, and trade restrictions could take away the former without restoring the latter. The idea of seizing control of the nation's economic destiny holds real popular appeal across the political spectrum, but it risks being an empty gesture with adverse economic consequences, undermining the legitimacy of a Fordist-style program going forward.

Even leaving aside the issue of trade, under a neo-Keynesian regime government spending would still be pumped into an economic system wired for neoliberalism. Obama's stimulus measure was a case in point. Though the stimulus arguably saved the United States from the deeper recession experienced in Europe, it did so at the price of expanding inequality even further relative to precrisis levels. This is because, while it was Keynesian to the extent that it started from the assumption that state spending could boost economic growth, it was operating within a neoliberal economic system—meaning that the very wealthy were in line to receive the lion's share of the benefits of that growth. One could anticipate perverse outcomes of other Fordist-style policies proposed by Sanders. Universal health care, for instance, could reduce resistance to the so-called gig economy by ameliorating one of the most serious consequences of unstable employment, namely uncertainty of access to health insurance. Free college tuition could also accelerate the process whereby a college degree, far from being a guaranteed path to class mobility, is increasingly a baseline expectation for any entry-level job. I would still support both policies, but they would not represent the kind of paradigm shift that the anti-neoliberal left is calling for.

I bring up these obstacles not to join the chorus of neoliberals proclaiming any return to Fordism impossible but to suggest the inadequacy of the framework within which such changes are typically advocated. That framework is a broadly Polanyian one in which the state (as representative of society) needs to push back against the excesses of the economy. On a superficial level it could appear to be the most radical possible reversal of neoliberalism's privileging of the economy over the state. Yet it strangely respects the division of labor established by neoliberal ideology, in which the economy maintains its autonomy and the state takes post hoc, indirect actions such as getting foreign competition out of the way, taxing away excessive incomes, or providing funding to give people access to the necessities of life. Again, such an agenda would doubtless be beneficial in many ways, but it would fail to match the ambition of neoliberal practice, which did not simply remove state interference from the economy, but transformed the state in order to enable it to support and cultivate new market forms.

Hence, though there are doubtless many beneficial reforms that could arise from such a framework, simply reversing neoliberalism's privileging of economy over state does not represent a paradigmatic shift. In fact, it risks simply deploying the *neoliberal* state over against a *neoliberal* economy, both of which were designed from the ground up to undo Fordism and render a return to it impossible. One cannot expect to rebuild Fordism using the instruments of its demolition—and among those instruments is the very division of labor between state and economy that shapes our contemporary common sense.

In terms of the question of durability, any attempt to reestablish something like the Fordist model would have to come to terms with that model's demise. In the previous chapter I remarked that neoliberalism appears to be in the process of failing to reproduce itself for the next generation. Essentially the same thing happened with Fordism. In fact, if we define Fordism as beginning at the end of the Second World War, then it proved even less durable, lasting approximately thirty years as compared to neoliberalism's forty or so (and counting). Doubtless, a major factor in its decline was the onset of an economic crisis caused by factors both exogenous (the oil crisis) and endogenous (the need to absorb the baby-boomer generation into the workforce), but neoliberalism has endured multiple crises of comparable magnitude. And though the shift to neoliberalism may appear all but inevitable in retrospect, there were also very plausible proposals to save the Fordist system by expanding the welfare apparatus rather than dismantling it.

There was, again, no historical necessity dictating that Fordism be replaced by neoliberalism. Yet just as the emergence of the right-wing reaction, while equally contingent, nonetheless gives us insight into the weaknesses and internal contradictions of neoliberalism, so too does the emergence of neoliberalism shed light on the vulnerabilities of Fordism. Peter Frase has recently articulated one major weakness of the Fordist system in terms of a Marxist critique of Polanyi.[4] From Polanyi's perspective, "Socialism is, essentially, the tendency inherent in an industrial civilization to transcend the self-regulating market by consciously subordinating it to a democratic society. It is the solution natural to industrial workers who see no reason why production should not be regulated directly and why markets should be more than a useful but subordinate trait in a free society."[5] In other words, in the long run the conflict between state (as representative of society) and market will settle into a steady equilibrium where social needs take the lead over market imperatives. Coming from a Marxist perspective, Frase asks, "Is that a stable equilibrium, acceptable to both capitalists and workers? Or is it an inherently unstable situation, one which must break toward either the expropriation of the capitalist class, or the restoration of ruling-class power?" The answer, he believes, is the latter. Though there is a convincing case to be made that "putting unemployed workers back to work would be good for capitalists too, in the sense that it would lead to faster growth and more profits," such purely economic arguments miss the point that the relationship between boss and worker is not solely economic but political—it is not just about making money, but about power and control.

Here Frase is drawing on the predictions of Michal Kalecki—who published his classic essay "Political Aspects of Full Employment" in 1943,[6] the year before *The Great Transformation* and *The Road to Serfdom* appeared—that any reform movement to strengthen the hand of workers within the capitalist system will eventually create a dynamic that, in Frase's words, "calls into question not just profits, but the underlying property relations of capitalism itself." That prediction came true throughout the Western world in the late 1960s and early 1970s, which witnessed a proliferation of strike actions and the emergence of demands to vastly expand the welfare state. Perhaps most radical, from a Marxist perspective, was the proposal to institute a universal basic income, which would break with the basic premise of the capitalist system by decoupling income from labor for the entire population rather than for the capitalist class alone. Once this critical moment, which Frase calls the "Kalecki point," is reached, "employers become willing to take drastic action to get workers back into line, even at the expense of short-term profitability," including "a 'capital strike' in which money is moved overseas or simply left in the bank, as a way of breaking the power of the working class."

To put this argument in the political theological terms of the previous chapter, the Fordist welfare state could be conceived as a restrainer or *katechon*, holding back the depredations of the market—an analogy that is all the more fitting in that Polanyi so frequently figures the market in demonic terms. The irony, though, is that the very means by which Fordist policy makers believed they were permanently containing the dangers of unrestrained capitalism actually guaranteed that a decisive crisis would emerge, a crisis that the Polanyian framework rendered all but unthinkable.

And here we come to another irony of the emergence of neoliberalism. In the United States, at least, Fordism was dismantled with the enthusiastic complicity of the very population that most benefited from it: white working- and middle-class homeowners, the so-called Reagan Democrats. As we saw in the previous chapter, Cooper has shown how emergent neoliberalism was able to mobilize anxieties and resentments relating to gender relations, sexual practice, and racial hierarchy in order to recruit such privileged populations into the neoliberal tax revolt. The very "household" norms that had once served to shore up the legitimacy of the welfare state were now turned against it, as the populations who had historically been excluded from its protections were perversely identified as its sole beneficiaries. Here again, we see a weak spot in the Polanyian framework, within which these "household" factors would be grouped on the side of society as opposed to economy. Drawing on Federici, however, my analysis has shown that the gendered division of labor, the disciplining of sexuality, and the enforcement of racial hierarchy have been intrinsic to the capitalist system from the very beginning—meaning that the Fordist project was paradoxically attempting to use the favored tools of capitalism in order to restrain capitalism.

Overall, then, the order that presented itself as restraining and controlling capitalism was actually deeply dependent on it. This is true at the most basic political theological level, since Fordism staked its legitimacy on continuous economic growth. That doubtless seemed a safe bet in the immediate postwar decades, but it took only one protracted economic crisis—one that was, by contemporary standards, relatively mild—to call the legitimacy of the entire system into question. Once the promise of endless prosperity appeared to be broken, conditions were ripe for neoliberals, in alliance with neoconservatives, to portray the welfare state as a parasitic institution that supported social parasites, legitimating their effort to dismantle welfare programs and transform them from a safety net into a disciplinary apparatus.

And the worst part was that these accusations were not entirely false. The social democratic institutions of the Fordist era really were parasitical on capitalist production, in that they used the state's power of taxation to take a substantial share of capitalist profits and redistribute them. Those redistribution projects themselves depended on capitalist production, because the money they provided was only helpful in that it allowed people to purchase goods and services in the capitalist marketplace. The Fordist system was thus in the awkward position of abrogating capitalist property rights—above all in the punitive tax rates for higher income levels—while still depending on the capitalist system's continued operation. Though I view such measures as justified and desirable, they were intrinsically vulnerable to attacks on their legitimacy, particularly because gender, sexual, and racial hierarchies opened up the possibility that the bulk of the population could be induced to identify with the property owners whose wealth was being expropriated rather than with the beneficiaries of the system.

The core vulnerability of Fordism was that for all its regulation of and intervention into the economy, it did not take the step of fully transforming the economy—either in the contemporary sense of the mode of production or in the more ancient sense of the organization of the household. From this perspective, Hardt and Negri have argued that neoliberalism and social democracy share the same defect. The neoliberal regime can do nothing but extract wealth, and social democracy, even with its very different ends, does the same: neither can "fulfill . . . the task of promoting, managing, and regulating production."[7] Both merely siphon off value, whether for investment capital or social services, but neither takes responsibility for directly producing value.

More than Sanders, Corbyn pushes in this direction when he advocates renationalizing industries (such as the railways) that were privatized under neoliberalism. And in this Corbyn represents an older tradition on the Labour left that called for state ownership and management of firms and even entire industries, a tradition that has its counterparts throughout Western Europe. While neoliberal dogma presents such regimes as inherently inefficient and oppressive, they were in fact compatible with higher sustained economic growth and more broadly shared increases in standards of living than we have seen in the neoliberal era. Even in the Soviet bloc, for all the mounting problems with the central planning model, what brought about the regime's demise was not an economic collapse but the decision on the part of the country's own political elites to dissolve the Union and convert to a capitalist system. And when the post-Soviet leadership submitted to the economic "shock therapy" recommended by Western advisers, the result was an immediate, and thus far permanent, decline in living standards for the vast majority of the population, accompanied by an explosion of wealth for a small elite.

In short, the world has already witnessed functional regimes that combined varying degrees of consciously planned economic production, guided by varying levels of democratic accountability. Not all such regimes are equally appealing as models for contemporary economic transformation, but all point toward the possibility of taking back control from the invisible hand. The experience of the neoliberal era shows us, even if only negatively, that this form of control is the most important of all—far more than the illusory goal of taking back control over our national destiny, for example.

Toward a World Come of Age

A break with the invisible hand would represent a return to the aspirations of the modern world that are most promising, aspirations that were perhaps best recognized, ironically enough, by a Christian theologian. Writing in 1944 from his jail cell in Tegel—where he was imprisoned for his role in a failed assassination attempt against Hitler and where he would be summarily executed by the Nazis just prior to the Allied victory—Dietrich Bonhoeffer embarked on a series of increasingly radical reflections on the place of Christianity in the modern world.[8] These fragments have proven durably influential and controversial in postwar theological debates, due in part to Bonhoeffer's fate as a kind of modern martyr, but in this context, what is most relevant is his interpretation of modernity. In his letter of June 8, 1944, to his friend and acolyte Eberhard Bethge, Bonhoeffer writes:

> The movement that began about the thirteenth century (I'm not going to get involved in any argument about the exact date) towards the autonomy of man (in which I should include the discovery of the laws by which the world lives and deals with itself in science, social and political matters, art, ethics, and religion) has in our time reached an undoubted completion. Man has learned to deal with himself in all questions of importance without recourse to the "working hypothesis" called "God." (325)

Christian polemics against this development have proven fruitless, because they refuse to recognize how much things have changed:

> The world that has become conscious of itself and the laws that govern its own existence has grown self-confident in what seems to us to be an uncanny way. False developments and failures do not make the world doubt the necessity of the course that it is taking, or of its development; they are accepted with fortitude and detachment as part of the bargain, and even an event like the present war is no exception. (326)

That such a seemingly optimistic reflection on the modern world should be written in a Nazi prison may seem ironic, but as a Christian theologian (indeed, from many perspectives a very conservative one), Bonhoeffer is well aware that human autonomy does not necessarily produce positive results. His main goal, however, is not to castigate the modern world for its sins—

not even for the sins that drove him to break with his pacifist principles in a desperate attempt to stop them—but to encourage Christians to embrace the new reality of a "world come of age" rather than fighting a losing battle to return to a world that could not live without God.

Against Christians who react with horror to Nietzsche's proclamation of the "death of God," then, Bonhoeffer is asking Christians to find a way to live in a world where God really is dead. And had he lived to see it, he would surely view it as deeply ironic that the modern world would construct its own replacement god. For that is ultimately what happened, as neoliberal technocrats set about the hard work of constructing and maintaining the market mechanism, essentially resurrecting an artificial invisible hand that they passed off as an unquestionable, quasi-divine authority.

If Bonhoeffer was right to detect in modern history "one great development that leads to the world's autonomy" (359), then the victory-by-default of neoliberalism in the early 1990s really did represent the end of history. It was the end of any notion that human beings should or could create their own destiny, the end of any notion of collective deliberation and decision making on ultimate questions. Liberal democracy under neoliberalism represents a forced choice between two fundamentally similar options, betraying its promise to provide a mechanism for rational and self-reflective human agency. The market similarly mobilizes free choice only to subdue and subvert it, "responsibilizing" every individual for the outcomes of the system while radically foreclosing any form of collective responsibility for the shape of society. And any attempt to exercise human judgment and free choice over social institutions and outcomes is rejected as a step down the slippery slope to totalitarianism. To choose in any strong sense is always necessarily to choose wrongly, to fall into sin.

Yet this end of history, this evacuation of freedom, was in the last analysis collectively chosen, if only passively. This means that—contrary to Wendy Brown's vision of a world in which democratic aspirations would be extinguished for good—the option of rejecting the hollow neoliberal vision of human freedom has always been on the table. Our present political moment is the beginning of a struggle to withdraw consent from the neoliberal order by developing a new and more meaningful conception of freedom. This initial gesture of refusal is an absolutely necessary first step, clearing the space to imagine something new. More work is needed, however, because at this early stage, the alternative conceptions of freedom can be characterized more by what they reject than by what they promote. Both demand freedom *from* neoliberalism (construed in different ways), but neither is quite clear on what they want freedom *for*.

For the right, freedom means freedom from foreign interference, which ultimately means freedom from the global economic forces that infringe on national sovereignty. Such a conception of freedom clearly holds popular appeal. Yet it is hobbled, not only by its addiction to nostalgia and magical thinking, but even more so by its lack of any positive goal. When these movements do seize power and assert their precious freedom, it is revealed to be an empty gesture of defiance with no program of its own. What is the point of Brexit, for instance, or of Obamacare repeal? There is ultimately no answer aside from the tautology that they must do it because they said they would do it. They have done and will continue to do profound damage, but the right-wing alternative as currently construed is a dead end that does not open out onto any real positive project.

Much more promising are the proposals on the left, where freedom means freedom from exploitation and precarity—which is to say, from the anxiety that has become pandemic in the neoliberal age. At its most ambitious, contemporary social democracy pictures a world in which a universal basic income will free us from the compulsion to sell our labor power on the market. Such a world would be very different from the one we live in now, and in my opinion much more desirable. Yet without a positive conception of collective freedom to match its negative conception of individual freedom, it would remain as vulnerable to overthrow as the Fordist paradigm. This is because neoliberalism, unlike its emerging rivals, actually does have some minimal positive conception of freedom: the freedom to participate in the market. As hollow as it may seem, in a capitalist society market freedom is undeniably a very important freedom, because the market is where all our material needs are met. No matter how many institutions we develop to redirect or correct market forces, no matter how big a cut society takes from market profits, a society that relies on the workings of the invisible hand to supply the most nonnegotiable social goods is still fundamentally a market society. And that means that, even if the state or some other institutional form can supply a positive alternative, market freedom will remain the tacit foundation of the social order by default, a ticking time-bomb waiting to explode into another neoliberal "end of history."

This means that any political theological paradigm that desires a real break with neoliberalism must be willing to break with the foundational role of the market. It must be willing to take responsibility for consciously and collectively directing the production and distribution of economic goods. Such a society may have room for a free market in discretionary consumer goods, but it would not allow what it considers to be its nonnegotiable needs and desires to be held hostage to profit-seeking individuals and firms. If some form of production must happen, if some need must be met, if some important cultural touchstone should be preserved, then such a society would mobilize the resources necessary to make it happen. Market mechanisms may be useful in some contexts,[9] but they must be designed to serve social ends directly rather than creating a profit incentive and hoping the social end is served along the way. None of this is to say that total conscious control of the production process is possible or desirable, but the limits to that control must be discovered through experimentation rather than read off of economic models that were designed to naturalize the capitalist system. From that perspective, it does not matter whether the forms of collective action that direct production are conceived as belonging to the "state" or the "economy"—in fact, the practice of collective deliberation about production would represent the most durable possible break with that foundational binary of the modern world.

Neoliberal ideology has conditioned us all to be suspicious of any prospect for deliberate, conscious social change. It is easy to imagine the objections: "Who decides what must be produced? Who decides who gets what?" When people ask questions like that, they normally do not anticipate any possible answer. "Who decides?" is a rhetorical question, meant to end a discussion, not open one up—as though the idea of collective deliberation and action, in and of itself, is an unthinkable horror.

It is worth reflecting on this reflex reaction, which is a result of ideological formation but cannot be reduced to that. I have claimed that the political theological root of neoliberalism is freedom and have characterized its vision of freedom as hollow. Yet paradoxically, part of the appeal of neoliberalism is precisely the limitation it places on freedom. While from a certain point of view it illegitimately "responsibilizes" us for outcomes that are beyond our control, from another perspective it relieves us of collective responsibility—with all the political conflict and struggle that meaningful collective action brings with it. Even beyond the promise of superior economic outcomes, the invisible hand allows us to imagine that we can outsource our collective responsibility to a machinelike entity that will deliver outcomes that are no one's fault because they are everyone's fault. On the political theological level, it is a conflict-avoidance mechanism as much as and perhaps even more than an economic mechanism, but like every *katechon*, it has inevitably generated the very forces of conflict it hoped to stave off indefinitely.

Dismantling the invisible hand is a crucial step toward creating a new political-theological paradigm, but it is not sufficient in itself. We will need to work simultaneously to radically reconceive the economy in the most ancient sense of the household: the order of race, gender, and sexual practice. We must not assume that a reimagining of the economy will automatically achieve this, as some simplistic forms of Marxism claim. As Polanyi documents, the Fascist social order was in many respects a transformation of the market society, but the structures of race, gender, and sexual practice, far from falling away of their own accord, became unimaginably more virulent and destructive. Closer to home, we have also seen how the conservative sexual and racial mores of Fordism ultimately allowed most of its social-democratic gains to be undone, paving the way for a neoliberal state devoted to reinforcing racial hierarchy by consigning racialized populations to the hell of the carceral system. The division between economic and social problems is a dangerous illusion—both must be tackled together, without indulging the illusion that there is any pre-existing standard for how either should be arranged.

Clearly, the task of building a new political-theological paradigm to replace neoliberalism is a massive one, for which there are no ready-made formulas. I promised that this conclusion would provide us with ways to recognize a genuinely new political theological paradigm when it comes, but the only infallible sign I can offer is that we will know that it is a new paradigm when we find ourselves building it. We will know that something genuinely new is in the offing when we recognize ourselves—in the broadest possible sense, with the full participation and leadership from the groups that neoliberalism subordinates and scapegoats—as part of a movement to form a social order that pursues goals that we have collectively chosen via means that we have collaboratively created. And we will know that we have truly embarked on this path when we can accept what the false idol of the omniscient market promised to eliminate: the irreducibility of political conflict. We must not imagine that agreement will automatically result if ideological blinders (such as categories of race, gender, or sexuality) or other extrinsic obstacles are removed, nor should we think that the people's will, when truly expressed, necessarily carries with it positive results.

Both these fantasies rest on the idea that, underneath it all, the interests of the people and the means to those ends are objectively determinable. Yet the ultimate lesson of political theology is that no such final answer exists. We are always thrown back on our own devices. Human beings *must* create their own structures of meaning and legitimacy because there is no one else who can create them. Even if a structure of meaning and legitimacy did come down from heaven, we would still have to decide whether to accept it, and there would doubtless be considerable conflict and dissent around the question. Meaning and legitimacy are irreducibly human products, and that means that they are inevitably the result of human creativity, struggle, and conflict. Harnessing, taming, and (where possible) resolving that conflict will take more than elections or consumer choices—those centuries-old decision-making technologies that at best represent training wheels for a "world come of age"—and it may well take more than debate and persuasion. We will need to confront the question of "who decides" as a genuine question rather than a rhetorical conversation-stopper.

In the end, though, I cannot claim to know exactly what will be required or what the end result will look like, nor can anyone else. What I do know is that the alternative is to live in a world where we are continually entrapped into endorsing our own exploitation and subordination, a world where we are forced into complicity with oppression and irreversible environmental destruction. It would be more comfortable to believe that the invisible hand will find a way out or that the forces of historical progress will rescue us. Yet surely, at this late date, we can recognize that those Gods are just as dead as their medieval predecessor. And what I want to suggest in closing is that this fact is not to be lamented, but embraced. The political theological paradigm of the future will not seek to resurrect a dead God, but will start from the premise that no one can deliver us from this body of death but us.

NOTES

Introduction

1. Adam Kotsko, *The Prince of This World* (Stanford: Stanford University Press, 2016).

2. Karl Polanyi, *The Great Transformation: The Political and Economic Origins of Our Time* (Boston: Beacon, 2001).

3. Carl Schmitt, *Political Theology: Four Chapters on the Concept of Sovereignty*, trans. George Schwab (Chicago: University of Chicago Press, 2005); Ernst Kantorowicz, *The King's Two Bodies: A Study in Medieval Political Theology* (Princeton, NJ: Princeton University Press, 2016).

4. Louis Althusser, "Ideology and Ideological State Apparatuses (Notes Towards an Investigation)," in *Lenin and Philosophy and Other Essays*, trans. Ben Brewster (New York: Monthly Review Press, 1971), 189–219.

5. Will Davies, *The Limits of Neoliberalism: Authority, Sovereignty, and the Logic of Competition*, rev. ed. (Los Angeles: Sage, 2017), xxii.

6. Davies is a notable exception to this rule, as he makes frequent reference to the necessity of state action to neoliberalism and, in fact, explicitly cites Schmitt's theory of sovereign emergency powers throughout *The Limits of Neoliberalism*.

Chapter 1

1. Perhaps the most widely read recent example is George Monbiot, "Neoliberalism—The Ideology at the Root of All Our Problems," *Guardian*, April 15, 2016, www.theguardian.com/books/2016/apr/15/neoliberalism-ideology-problem-george-monbiot.

2. Milton Friedman, "Neo-Liberalism and Its Prospects," in *The Indispensable Milton Friedman: Essays on Politics and Economics*, ed. Lanny Ebenstein (Washington, DC:

Regnery, 2012), 3–9; subsequent citations will be given in-text. I owe this reference to Dotan Leshem.

3. Philip Mirowski, *Never Let a Serious Crisis Go to Waste: How Neoliberalism Survived the Financial Meltdown* (New York: Verso, 2013).

4. David Harvey, *A Brief History of Neoliberalism* (New York: Oxford University Press, 2005).

5. Harvey, *Brief History*, 3.

6. See Harvey, *Brief History*, chap. 5. For an argument that China has diverged substantially from the neoliberal path, see Giovanni Arrighi, *Adam Smith in Beijing: Lineages of the Twenty-First Century* (New York: Verso, 2007), 353–61.

7. See Pierrot Dardot and Christian Laval's critique in *The New Way of the World: On Neoliberal Society*, trans. Gregory Elliott (New York: Verso, 2013), 9.

8. Wendy Brown, *Undoing the Demos: Neoliberalism's Stealth Revolution* (Cambridge: Zone, 2015).

9. Jodi Dean, *Democracy and Other Neoliberal Fantasies: Communicative Capitalism and Left Politics* (Durham, NC: Duke University Press, 2009).

10. Michel Foucault, *The Birth of Biopolitics: Lectures at the Collège de France, 1978–79*, trans. Graham Burchell (New York: Picador, 2008).

11. This holds not only in Jodi Dean's work but also in Mark Fisher's *Capitalist Realism* (New York: Zero, 2008), which remains perhaps our best account of how it *feels* to live under neoliberalism.

12. This is the case also for Maurizio Lazzarato's analysis of neoliberalism in terms of Deleuze and Guattari in *The Making of the Indebted Man: An Essay on the Neoliberal Condition*, trans. Joshua David Jordan (Los Angeles: Semiotext(e), 2012), insofar as he emphasizes Deleuze and Guattari's continuity with both Marx and Foucault.

13. One of the only major attempts to use political theology as a lens for grasping neoliberalism is Eric Santner, *The Weight of All Flesh: On the Subject-Matter of Political Economy*, ed. Kevis Goodman (New York: Oxford University Press, 2016). It is evocative enough to amply demonstrate the promise of this approach, but it represents only a preliminary presentation of Santner's project in the form of published lectures.

14. Jacob Taubes, *The Political Theology of Paul*, ed. Aleia Assmann and Jan Assmann, trans. Dana Hollander (Stanford: Stanford University Press, 2004), 16.

15. Schmitt, *Political Theology*, 36.

16. See Walter Benjamin, "Capitalism as Religion," trans. Rodney Livingston, in *Selected Writings*, vol. 1, *1913–1926*, ed. Marcus Bullock and Michael W. Jennings (Cambridge, MA: Harvard University Press, 1996), 288–91.

17. See John D. Caputo, *Prayers and Tears of Jacques Derrida: Religion Without Religion* (Bloomington: Indiana University Press, 1997); Michael Naas, *Derrida from Now On* (New York: Fordham University Press, 2008); and Martin Hägglund, *Radical Atheism: Derrida and the Time of Life* (Stanford: Stanford University Press, 2008).

18. Schmitt, *Political Theology*, 5.

19. See Giorgio Agamben, *Homo Sacer: Sovereign Power and Bare Life*, trans. David Heller-Roazen (Stanford: Stanford University Press, 1998). The Italian text was originally published in 1995, but Agamben had discussed the figure of the *homo sacer*, or sacred man (who may be killed with impunity but not sacrificed), as early as *Language and Death: The Place of Negativity*, trans. Karen Pinkus and Michael Hardt (Minneapolis: University of Minnesota Press, 1991), which originally appeared in 1982.

20. Michael Hardt and Antonio Negri, *Commonwealth* (Cambridge, MA: Belknap Press/Harvard University Press, 2009), §4.1.

21. Hardt and Negri, *Commonwealth*, 203–4.

22. Hardt and Negri, *Commonwealth*, 4.

23. Hardt and Negri, *Commonwealth*, 5.

24. Giorgio Agamben, *The Kingdom and the Glory: For a Theological Genealogy of Economy and Government*, trans. Lorenzo Chiesa and Matteo Mandarini (Stanford: Stanford University Press, 2011).

25. I argue that *The Kingdom and the Glory* and Agamben's subsequent theologically oriented works are concerned with neoliberalism in specific in "The Theology of Neoliberalism," in Colby Dickinson and Adam Kotsko, *Agamben's Coming Philosophy: Finding a New Use for Theology* (New York: Rowman and Littlefield International, 2015), 183–200.

26. See Harvey, *Brief History*, 29, 73.

27. Harvey, *Brief History*, 85.

28. See Joshua Ramey, *Politics of Divination: Neoliberal Endgame and the Religion of Contingency* (New York: Rowman and Littlefield International, 2016); and Joseph Vogl, *Specters of Capital*, trans. Joachim Redner and Robert Savage (Stanford: Stanford University Press, 2014).

29. See Mark C. Taylor, *Confidence Games: Money and Markets in a World Without Redemption* (Chicago: University of Chicago Press, 2004).

30. Brown, *Undoing the Demos*, 216.

31. Brown, *Undoing the Demos*, 218.

32. Brown, *Undoing the Demos*, 210. Ramey expands on Brown's comments to claim that neoliberalism is a political theology (see *Politics of Divination*, 151), but he does so in the more narrow sense that I am attempting to break with here.

33. Will Davies's *Limits of Neoliberalism* is again an exception to this generalization because he defines neoliberalism as "the disenchantment of politics by economics" (6)—in other words, as a transformation of politics, not an abolition or simply shunting aside of politics—and argues that the disturbing thing about the emergency measures taken around the financial crisis was not that they used state power as such, but that they suspended the previously nonnegotiable rules of economic policy (chap. 5).

34. This connection between neoliberalism and neoconservatism on the level of

practical politics in the United States has been masterfully documented in Melinda Cooper, *Family Values: Between Neoliberalism and the New Social Conservatism* (New York: Zone, 2017).

35. Carl Schmitt, *The Concept of the Political*, trans. George Schwab (Chicago: University of Chicago Press, 1996), 26.

36. Schmitt, *Concept of the Political*, 27.

37. Schmitt, *Concept of the Political*, 48.

38. Schmitt, *Concept of the Political*, 49.

39. Schmitt, *Concept of the Political*, 49.

40. Schmitt, *Political Theology*, 5.

41. Schmitt, *Concept of the Political*, 35.

42. Schmitt, *Political Theology*, 15.

43. Schmitt, *Concept of the Political*, 78.

44. See Schmitt, *Political Theology*, 63–64.

45. Schmitt, *Political Theology*, 36.

46. Schmitt, *Political Theology*, 45.

47. Schmitt, *Political Theology*, 45–46.

48. See Paul Tillich, *Dynamics of Faith* (New York: Harper Perennial, 2009). My use of this term is inspired by Philip Goodchild's approach in *Theology of Money* (Durham, NC: Duke University Press, 2007).

49. I have traced one historical trajectory of the intertwining of the problem of evil and the problem of legitimacy in *The Prince of This World*. There, for the sake of convenience, I chose to designate particular historical approaches to the problem of political theology as "paradigms," a practice I will continue in the present volume.

50. Schmitt, *Political Theology*, 51.

51. Schmitt, *Political Theology*, 50.

52. Foucault, *Birth of Biopolitics*, 187.

53. Foucault, *Birth of Biopolitics*, 82.

54. Foucault, *Birth of Biopolitics*, 83.

55. Foucault, *Birth of Biopolitics*, 94–95.

Chapter 2

1. Dardot and Laval, *New Way of the World*, 7.

2. Dardot and Laval, *New Way of the World*, 9.

3. Dardot and Laval, *New Way of the World*, 9.

4. Dardot and Laval, *New Way of the World*, 12.

5. Ernesto Laclau and Chantal Mouffe, *Hegemony and Socialist Strategy: Towards a Radical Democratic Politics*, 2nd ed. (New York: Verso, 2014).

6. The classic articulation of Žižek's position remains his first major publication, *The Sublime Object of Ideology* (New York: Verso, 1989). For my account of the development

of his thought over the subsequent two decades, see Adam Kotsko, *Žižek and Theology* (New York: Clark, 2008).

7. In particular, I take from Žižek the conviction that human social orders are responding to a fundamentally unfixable problem (what he calls the Lacanian Real and I call deadlock underlying the problem of evil or problem of legitimacy), that therefore no solution to this problem can claim to be complete or fully self-consistent (in Lacanian terms, every symbolic order is *pas-tout*, non-all or non-whole), and that we need an account of what "hooks" people and convinces them to go along with the social order. Hence on a purely formal level, one could say that my general political theology is very "Žižekian."

8. In this sense he falls victim to Dardot and Laval's critique of Marxism: his body of work is increasingly characterized by "the sheer repetition of the same scenarios, with the same characters in new costumes and the same plots in new settings" (*New Way of the World*, 7). For an encapsulation of my growing ambivalence toward Žižek's project see Adam Kotsko, "Repetition and Regression: The Problem of Christianity and Žižek's 'Middle Period,'" in *Repeating Žižek*, ed. Agon Hamza (Durham, NC: Duke University Press, 2015).

9. See, e.g., Daniel Zamora and Michael C. Bennett, eds., *Foucault and Neoliberalism* (New York: Polity, 2015).

10. Brown, *Undoing the Demos*, 17 (emphasis in original). Subsequent citations will be given in-text.

11. Schmitt, *Concept of the Political*, 78.

12. Jodi Dean, *Crowds and Party* (New York: Verso, 2016).

13. See Dean, *Democracy and Other Neoliberal Fantasies*, chaps. 3, 4, and 6, respectively.

14. Dean, *Democracy and Other Neoliberal Fantasies*, 1.

15. Hannah Arendt, *The Human Condition*, 2nd ed. (Chicago: University of Chicago Press, 1958). Subsequent citations will be given in-text.

16. See Adriel M. Trott, "Nature, Action, and Politics: A Critique of Arendt's Reading of Aristotle," *Ancient Philosophy* 37, no. 1 (2017): 113–28.

17. Aristotle, *Politics*, trans. Joe Sachs (Newburyport, MA: Focus, 2012), 23 (bk. 1, chap. 13).

18. Aristotle, *Politics*, 25 (bk. 1, chap. 13).

19. Aristotle, *Politics*, 26 (bk. 1, chap. 13).

20. Aristotle, *Politics*, 2 (bk. 1, chap. 2).

21. Aristotle, *Politics*, 4 (bk. 1, chap. 2).

22. Aristotle, *Politics*, 5 (bk. 1, chap. 2).

23. Trott, "Nature, Action, and Politics," 127.

24. Agamben, *Homo Sacer*, 1 (Greek transliteration altered).

25. Jacques Derrida, *The Beast and the Sovereign*, vol. 1, trans. Geoffrey Bennington (Chicago: University of Chicago Press, 2009), 92–95.

26. Agamben, *Homo Sacer*, 3.

27. Agamben, *Homo Sacer*, 4.

28. Giorgio Agamben, *State of Exception*, trans. Kevin Attell (Chicago: University of Chicago Press, 2005). This is in many ways a Heideggerian revision of Arendt's already very Heideggerian narrative: what appears to be a distinctively modern problem actually has its root in the Greek "forgetting of Being" (initiated in Plato) and in the transition to Roman hegemony.

29. Giorgio Agamben, *The Use of Bodies*, trans. Adam Kotsko (Stanford: Stanford University Press, 2016), pt. 1 passim.

30. Giorgio Agamben, *The Sacrament of Language*, trans. Adam Kotsko (Stanford: Stanford University Press, 2011), 72.

31. Agamben, *The Kingdom and the Glory*, xi (translation altered for inclusive language). Subsequent citations will be given in-text.

32. Dotan Leshem, *The Origins of Neoliberalism: Modeling the Economy from Jesus to Foucault* (New York: Columbia University Press, 2016). Subsequent citations will be given in-text.

33. See Kotsko, "The Theology of Neoliberalism."

34. Marie-José Mondzain, *Image, Icon, Economy: The Byzantine Origins of the Contemporary Imaginary*, trans. Rico Franses (Stanford: Stanford University Press, 2005).

35. Mondzain, *Image, Icon, Economy*, xii.

36. Mondzain, *Image, Icon, Economy*, 61.

37. Mondzain, *Image, Icon, Economy*, 6.

38. Her claim of contemporary relevance is every bit as bold as Leshem's claim to have uncovered "the origins of neoliberalism"—indeed, perhaps even more so, since she is making a case for "the Byzantine origins of the contemporary imaginary."

39. Taylor, *Confidence Games*, 213.

40. Taylor, *Confidence Games*, xi–xiv.

41. Taylor, *Confidence Games*, xvi.

42. Goodchild, *Theology of Money*, 166.

43. Goodchild, *Theology of Money*, 168–69.

44. Ramey, *Politics of Divination*, vii.

45. Ramey, *Politics of Divination*, 7.

46. Ramey, *Politics of Divination*, 7.

47. Ramey twice describes neoliberalism as a "political theology" (*Politics of Divination*, 6, 151), but he does not define the term and, as discussed briefly in the previous chapter, he seems to me to use it inconsistently or perhaps metaphorically.

48. Ramey, *Politics of Divination*, 3.

49. Ramey, *Politics of Divination*, chap. 2.

50. See Eric Santner, *The Royal Remains: The People's Two Bodies and the Endgames of Sovereignty* (Chicago: University of Chicago Press, 2011).

51. Santner, *Weight of All Flesh*, 80.

52. Friedrich Nietzsche, *Genealogy of Morals*, in *Basic Writings of Nietzsche*, trans. and ed. Walter Kaufmann (New York: Modern Library, 1992), 513; "Second Essay," §12.

53. Aristotle, *Politics*, 18 (bk. 1, chap. 9).

54. Polanyi, *The Great Transformation*, 56.

Chapter 3

1. Polanyi, *The Great Transformation*, 147.

2. Cooper, *Family Values*, 13. Subsequent citations will be given in-text.

3. See Cooper, *Family Values*, chap. 2 in particular.

4. Aristotle, *Politics*, 10 (bk. 1, chap. 5).

5. Cooper, *Family Values*, 97.

6. See Polanyi, *The Great Transformation*, chap. 7.

7. Polanyi, *The Great Transformation*, 164.

8. Polanyi, *The Great Transformation*, 164.

9. Polanyi, *The Great Transformation*, 164–65.

10. Polanyi, *The Great Transformation*, 166.

11. Silvia Federici, *Caliban and the Witch: Women, the Body, and Primitive Accumulation*, 2nd ed. (New York: Autonomedia, 2014), 9.

12. Federici, *Caliban and the Witch*, 17 (emphasis added).

13. For this latter process see the chapter "Colonization and Christianization" in particular.

14. Federici, *Caliban and the Witch*, 239.

15. Heinrich Kramer and James Sprenger, *Malleus Maleficarum*, trans. Montague Summers (New York: Dover, 1971).

16. A partial catalogue of the witches' sins runs as follows: "First, by inclining the minds of men to inordinate passion; second, by obstructing their generative force; third, by removing the members accommodated to that act; fourth, by changing men into beasts by their magic art; fifth, by destroying the generative force in women; sixth, by procuring abortion; seventh, by offering children to devils . . ." (Kramer and Sprenger, *Malleus Maleficarum*, 47).

17. Kramer and Sprenger, *Malleus Maleficarum*, 68.

18. See the reference to Jodi Dean's analysis in the previous chapter, page 47.

19. Cooper, *Family Values*, 295 (emphasis in original).

20. Cooper, *Family Values*, 299.

21. For a sympathetic account of American Pentecostalism that laments its descent into the prosperity gospel, see Harvey Cox, *Fire from Heaven: The Rise of Pentecostal Spirituality and the Reshaping of Religion in the Twenty-First Century* (Cambridge: Da Capo, 1995).

22. See, e.g., Paul Gifford, *Ghana's New Christianity: Pentecostalism in a Globalizing African Economy*, new ed. (Bloomington: Indiana University Press, 2004); and Kevin Lewis O'Neill, *Cities of God: Christian Citizenship in Postwar Guatemala* (Berkeley: University of California Press, 2009).

23. Agamben claims that "theology is itself 'economic' and did not simply become so at a later time through secularization" (*The Kingdom and the Glory*, 3) but embraces the notion of secularization when it comes to political concepts. It is difficult to understand why he draws this distinction, especially because (as I have shown in *The Prince of This World*, chap. 1), God is always already portrayed as a ruler and lawgiver in the biblical tradition; here, too, no process of "secularization" needs to intervene because theology is already political.

24. The account of divine providence and demonization that follows draws on and in some cases recapitulates my argument in *The Prince of This World*, particularly chaps. 4 and 5.

25. Augustine, *The City of God*, trans. Marcus Dods (New York: Modern Library, 1993), 11.23. Subsequent in-text references refer to book and chapter divisions.

26. Gregory of Nyssa, "An Address on Religious Instruction," ed. and trans. Cyril C. Richardson, in *Christology of the Later Fathers*, ed. Edward R. Hardy (Philadelphia: Westminster, 1954), §5.

27. Anselm of Canterbury, "On the Virgin Conception and Original Sin," in *The Major Works*, ed. Brian Davies and Gillian Evans (New York: Oxford University Press, 1998). Subsequent in-text citations refer to section numbers.

28. See Anselm, *Why God Became Man*, in *Major Works*.

29. See Gregory of Nyssa, "An Address," §§6–28.

30. See *City of God*, 11.9, where Augustine contends that in Genesis 1:3–5, the creation of light refers to the creation of all angels and the separation of light from darkness to the judgment of the rebellious angels.

31. See Polanyi, *The Great Transformation*, esp. 121–31.

32. Cooper, *Family Values*, 172.

33. Cooper, *Family Values*, 178.

34. Cooper, *Family Values*, 173 (emphasis in original).

35. Cooper, *Family Values*, 179.

36. Gary Becker, "Nobel Lecture: The Economic Way of Looking at Behavior," *Journal of Political Economy* 101, no. 3 (1993): 385–409. Subsequent citations given in-text.

37. The reference is to Richard H. Thayer and Cass R. Sunstein, *Nudge: Improving Decisions About Health, Wealth, and Happiness* (New Haven, CT: Yale University Press, 2008). Sunstein went on to play an important role in regulatory design for the Obama administration.

38. See Brown, *Undoing the Demos*, 10.

39. Michelle Alexander, *The New Jim Crow: Mass Incarceration in the Age of Colorblindness*, rev. ed. (New York: New Press, 2012). Subsequent references will be given in-text.

40. Here I draw on Santner's argument in *The Weight of All Flesh* that Marx's theory of surplus value is ultimately a theory of glory.

Chapter 4

1. Francis Fukuyama, "The End of History?" *National Interest*, Summer 1989, 1–18. Subsequent references will be given in-text.

2. Marika Rose, "After the Eschaton: *The Prince of This World* Book Event," *An und für sich*, April 27, 2017, https://itself.blog/2017/04/27/after-the-eschaton-the-prince-of-this-world-book-event.

3. Will Davies, "The New Neoliberalism," *New Left Review* 101 (Sept.-Oct. 2016): 121–34. Subsequent references will be given in-text. I owe this reference to Marika Rose.

4. Though the article was published after the Brexit vote, it does not mention Brexit, and Davies has confirmed to me that it was finalized before he could take that event into account.

5. David M. Herszenhorn, Carl Hulse, and Sheryl Gay Stolberg, "Talks Implode During a Day of Chaos; Fate of Bailout Plan Remains Unresolved," *New York Times*, Sept. 25, 2008, www.nytimes.com/2008/09/26/business/26bailout.html?mcubz=1.

6. For video of the rant, and excerpts of contemporaneous (strongly approving) reactions from conservative publications, see Eric Etheride, "Rick Santelli: Tea Party Time," *New York Times Opinionator*, Feb. 20, 2009, https://opinionator.blogs.nytimes.com/2009/02/20/rick-santelli-tea-party-time/?mcubz=1&_r=0.

7. See Lore Moore, "Rep. Todd Akin: The Statement and the Reaction," *New York Times*, August 20, 2012, www.nytimes.com/2012/08/21/us/politics/rep-todd-akin-legitimate-rape-statement-and-reaction.html?mcubz=1; and Patrick Marley, "Rep. Roger Rivard Criticized for 'Some Girls Rape Easy' Remark," *Milwaukee Journal-Sentinel*, Oct. 10, 2012, http://archive.jsonline.com/news/statepolitics/state-legislator-criticized-for-comments-on-rape-hj76f4k-173587961.html.

8. Tony Blair's New Labour also won an ever-decreasing plurality in every general election, starting with 1997, though I am less well-versed in the intricacies of UK politics and therefore less willing to make strong claims about the significance of this fact.

9. For an account and critique of the Trump infrastructure plan see Paul Krugman, "Infrastructure Build or Privatization Scam?" *The Conscience of a Liberal* (blog), *New York Times*, Nov. 19, 2016, https://krugman.blogs.nytimes.com/2016/11/19/infrastructure-build-or-privatization-scam/?mcubz=1.

10. Cooper, *Family Values*, 179.

11. This generalization only holds for heresies that arose after conventional ortho-

doxy was already well-established. Prior to that stage, one could characterize those who would retrospectively be viewed as orthodox as the conspiracy theorists, viewing those who disagreed about the meaning of the Christian message as members of a Satanic cult. See my discussion of Irenaeus in *The Prince of This World*, 62–70 passim.

12. For a detailed debunking of one such conspiracy theory see Sarah Jones, "Stop Promoting Liberal Conspiracy Theories on Twitter," *Minutes* (blog), *New Republic*, May 10, 2017, https://newrepublic.com/minutes/142650/stop-promoting-liberal-conspiracy-theories-twitter.

13. For the latter point, which at the time of this writing had received considerably less media attention than the other allegations, see Matthew Rosza, "Russia Attempted to Hack U.S. Voting Software Days Before Election: NSA Document," *Salon*, June 5, 2017, www.salon.com/2017/06/05/russia-attempted-to-hack-u-s-voting-software-days-before-election-nsa-document.

14. Dean, *Democracy and Other Neoliberal Fantasies*, 170.

15. Bryan Bender and Andrew Hanna, "Flynn Under Fire for Fake News: A Shooting at a D.C. Pizza Restaurant Is Stoking Criticism of the Conspiracy Theories Being Spread by Donald Trump's Pick for National Security Adviser," *Politico*, Dec. 5, 2016, www.politico.com/story/2016/12/michael-flynn-conspiracy-pizzeria-trump-232227.

16. For my account of the emergence of apocalyptic thought within the biblical tradition see *The Prince of This World*, chap. 1.

17. Friedrich Hayek, *The Road to Serfdom* (New York: Routledge, 2001).

18. All biblical quotations are taken from the New Revised Standard Version.

19. See the discussion in J. Christiaan Beker, *Heirs of Paul: Their Legacy in the New Testament and the Church Today* (Grand Rapids. MI: Eerdmans, 1991), 72–75.

20. Carl Schmitt, *The Nomos of the Earth in the International Law of the "Jus Publicum Europaeum,"* trans. and ed. G. L. Ulmen (New York: Telos, 2003), 59–66. Jacob Taubes subsequently argued that the concept was central to Schmitt's own political thought as well; see *To Carl Schmitt: Letters and Reflections*, trans. Keith Tribe (New York: Columbia University Press, 2013), 54.

21. I am among them: see *The Prince of This World*, chap. 5.

22. Cooper, *Family Values*, 245.

23. Brown, *Undoing the Demos*, 182.

24. Morgan Adamson, "The Human Capital Strategy," *Ephemera: Theory and Politics in Organization* 9, no. 4 (2009): 271–84.

25. For an analysis of neoliberalism centered entirely on debt, see Lazzarato, *The Making of the Indebted Man*. His emphasis on debt, not as a merely economic factor but, above all, as a power relation and mode of subject-formation, and his extended discussion of Nietzsche's *Genealogy of Morals*—necessarily entailing engagement with theology—both bring his project into close proximity with my political theology of

neoliberalism. The key difference is that I view debt as a symptom of the phenomenon of moral entrapment I call demonization rather than the root problem.

26. Lazzarato, *The Making of the Indebted Man*, 45–46.

27. See Lazzarato, *The Making of the Indebted Man*, 74 and passim.

28. I owe this insight to Vogl, *Specters of Capital*.

29. See Donald McKenzie, "End-of-the-World Trade," *London Review of Books*, May 8, 2008, 24–26, www.lrb.co.uk/v30/n09/donald-mackenzie/end-of-the-world-trade. Thank you to Kevin Sanchez for helping me track down this article.

30. Particularly striking is then-Federal Reserve Chair Alan Greenspan's refusal to acknowledge the possibility that multiple simultaneous local real-estate bubbles added up to a national bubble. See Edmund L. Andrews, "Greenspan Is Concerned About 'Froth' in Housing," *New York Times*, May 21, 2005, www.nytimes.com/2005/05/21/business/greenspan-is-concerned-about-froth-in-housing.html. I owe this reference to Mike Konczal.

31. Cooper, *Family Values*, 152.

Conclusion

1. This omission is all the more puzzling given that Schmitt published the initial versions of the essays that would become *Political Theology* in publications dedicated to Max Weber; see Taubes, *To Carl Schmitt*, 4.

2. Bonnie Honig, *Emergency Politics: Paradox, Law, Democracy* (Princeton, NJ: Princeton University Press, 2009), xv.

3. See Curt Mills, "Sanders Says He'll Work With Trump on Trade: Credit Earned with Liberals like Sanders Is Met with Hesitation by Some in Trump's Own Party," *U.S. News and World Report*, Jan. 24, 2017, www.usnews.com/news/politics/articles/2017-01-24/bernie-sanders-says-hell-work-with-trump-on-trade-while-some-gopers-wary.

4. Peter Frase, "Social Democracy's Breaking Point," *Jacobin*, June 30, 2016, unpaginated, www.jacobinmag.com/2016/06/social-democracy-polanyi-great-transformation-welfare-state.

5. Polanyi, *The Great Transformation*, 242.

6. Michal Kalecki, "Political Aspects of Full Employment," *Political Quarterly* 14, no. 4 (1943): 322–31.

7. Hardt and Negri, *Commonwealth*, 273.

8. Dietrich Bonhoeffer, *Letters and Papers from Prison*, ed. Eberhard Bethge, enl. ed. (New York: Touchstone, 1997). Subsequent citations will be given in-text.

9. Peter Frase discusses an experiment with market pricing of parking spaces, with the aim of guaranteeing a steady supply of spaces rather than making profit for a private investor, in *Four Futures: Life After Capitalism* (New York: Verso, 2016), 113–16.

BIBLIOGRAPHY

Adamson, Morgan. "The Human Capital Strategy." *Ephemera: Theory and Politics in Organization* 9, no. 4 (2009): 271–84.

Agamben, Giorgio. *Homo Sacer: Sovereign Power and Bare Life*. Translated by David Heller-Roazen. Stanford: Stanford University Press, 1998.

———. *The Kingdom and the Glory: For a Theological Genealogy of Economy and Government*. Translated by Lorenzo Chiesa and Matteo Mandarini. Stanford: Stanford University Press, 2011.

———. *Language and Death: The Place of Negativity*. Translated by Karen Pinkus and Michael Hardt. Minneapolis: University of Minnesota Press, 1991.

———. *The Sacrament of Language*. Translated by Adam Kotsko. Stanford: Stanford University Press, 2011.

———. *State of Exception*. Translated by Kevin Attell. Chicago: University of Chicago Press, 2005.

———. *The Use of Bodies*. Translated by Adam Kotsko. Stanford: Stanford University Press, 2016.

Alexander, Michelle. *The New Jim Crow: Mass Incarceration in the Age of Colorblindness*. Rev. ed. New York: New Press, 2012.

Althusser, Louis. "Ideology and Ideological State Apparatuses (Notes Towards an Investigation)." In *Lenin and Philosophy and Other Essays*. Translated by Ben Brewster. New York: Monthly Review Press, 1971.

Andrews, Edmund L. "Greenspan Is Concerned About 'Froth' in Housing." *New York Times*, May 21, 2005. www.nytimes.com/2005/05/21/business/greenspan-is-concerned-about-froth-in-housing.html.

Anselm of Canterbury. *The Major Works*. Edited by Brian Davies and Gillian Evans. New York: Oxford University Press, 1998.

Arendt, Hannah. *The Human Condition*. 2nd ed. Chicago: University of Chicago Press, 1958.

Aristotle. *Politics*. Translated by Joe Sachs. Newburyport, MA: Focus, 2012.

Arrighi, Giovanni. *Adam Smith in Beijing: Lineages of the Twenty-First Century*. New York: Verso, 2007.

Augustine. *The City of God*. Translated by Marcus Dods. New York: Modern Library, 1993.

Becker, Gary. "Nobel Lecture: The Economic Way of Looking at Behavior." *Journal of Political Economy* 101, no. 3 (1993): 385–409.

Beker, J. Christiaan. *Heirs of Paul: Their Legacy in the New Testament and the Church Today*. Grand Rapids, MI: Eerdmans, 1991.

Benjamin, Walter. "Capitalism as Religion." Translated by Rodney Livingston. In *Selected Writings*, vol. 1, *1913–1926*. Edited by Marcus Bullock and Michael W. Jennings. Cambridge, MA: Harvard University Press, 1996.

Bender, Bryan, and Andrew Hanna. "Flynn Under Fire for Fake News: A Shooting at a D.C. Pizza Restaurant Is Stoking Criticism of the Conspiracy Theories Being Spread by Donald Trump's Pick for National Security Adviser." *Politico*, Dec. 5, 2016. www.politico.com/story/2016/12/michael-flynn-conspiracy-pizzeria-trump-232227.

Bonhoeffer, Dietrich. *Letters and Papers from Prison*. Edited by Eberhard Bethge. Enl. ed. New York: Touchstone, 1997.

Brown, Wendy. *Undoing the Demos: Neoliberalism's Stealth Revolution*. Cambridge: Zone, 2015.

Caputo, John D. *Prayers and Tears of Jacques Derrida: Religion Without Religion*. Bloomington: Indiana University Press, 1997.

Cooper, Melinda. *Family Values: Between Neoliberalism and the New Social Conservatism*. New York: Zone, 2017.

Cox, Harvey. *Fire from Heaven: The Rise of Pentecostal Spirituality and the Reshaping of Religion in the Twenty-First Century*. Cambridge: Da Capo, 1995.

Dardot, Pierre, and Christian Laval. *The New Way of the World: On Neoliberal Society*. Translated by Gregory Elliott. New York: Verso, 2013.

Davies, Will. *The Limits of Neoliberalism: Authority, Sovereignty, and the Logic of Competition*. Rev. ed. Los Angeles: Sage, 2017.

———. "The New Neoliberalism." *New Left Review* 101 (Sept.-Oct. 2016): 121–34.

Dean, Jodi. *Crowds and Party*. New York: Verso, 2016.

———. *Democracy and Other Neoliberal Fantasies: Communicative Capitalism and Left Politics*. Durham, NC: Duke University Press, 2009.

Derrida, Jacques. *The Beast and the Sovereign*. Vol. 1. Translated by Geoffrey Bennington. Chicago: University of Chicago Press, 2009.

Etheride, Eric. "Rick Santelli: Tea Party Time." *New York Times Opinionator*. Feb. 20, 2009. https://opinionator.blogs.nytimes.com/2009/02/20/rick-santelli-tea-party-time/?mcubz=1&_r=0.

Federici, Silvia. *Caliban and the Witch: Women, the Body, and Primitive Accumulation*. 2nd ed. New York: Autonomedia, 2014.

Fisher, Mark. *Capitalist Realism*. New York: Zero, 2008.

Foucault, Michel. *The Birth of Biopolitics: Lectures at the Collège de France, 1978–79*. Translated by Graham Burchell. New York: Picador, 2008.

Frase, Peter. *Four Futures: Life After Capitalism*. New York: Verso, 2016.

———. "Social Democracy's Breaking Point." *Jacobin*, June 30, 2016. www.jacobinmag.com/2016/06/social-democracy-polanyi-great-transformation-welfare-state.

Friedman, Milton. "Neo-Liberalism and Its Prospects." In *The Indispensable Milton Friedman: Essays on Politics and Economics*, edited by Lanny Ebenstein, 3–9. Washington, DC: Regnery, 2012.

Fukuyama, Francis. "The End of History?" *National Interest*, Summer 1989, 1–18.

Gifford, Paul. *Ghana's New Christianity: Pentecostalism in a Globalizing African Economy*. New ed. Bloomington: Indiana University Press, 2004.

Goodchild, Philip. *Theology of Money*. Durham, NC: Duke University Press, 2007.

Gregory of Nyssa. "An Address on Religious Instruction." Edited and translated by Cyril C. Richardson. In *Christology of the Later Fathers*, edited by Edward R. Hardy, 268–325. Philadelphia: Westminster, 1954.

Hägglund, Martin. *Radical Atheism: Derrida and the Time of Life*. Stanford: Stanford University Press, 2008.

Hardt, Michael, and Antonio Negri. *Commonwealth*. Cambridge, MA: Belknap Press/Harvard University Press, 2009.

Harvey, David. *A Brief History of Neoliberalism*. New York: Oxford University Press, 2005.

Hayek, Friedrich. *The Road to Serfdom*. New York: Routledge, 2001.

Herszenhorn, David M., Carl Hulse, and Sheryl Gay Stolberg. "Talks Implode During a Day of Chaos; Fate of Bailout Plan Remains Unresolved." *New York Times*, Sept. 25, 2008. www.nytimes.com/2008/09/26/business/26bailout.html?mcubz=1.

Honig, Bonnie. *Emergency Politics: Paradox, Law, Democracy*. Princeton, NJ: Princeton University Press, 2009.

Jones, Sarah. "Stop Promoting Liberal Conspiracy Theories on Twitter." *Minutes* (blog). *New Republic*, May 10, 2017. https://newrepublic.com/minutes/142650/stop-promoting-liberal-conspiracy-theories-twitter.

Kalecki, Michal. "Political Aspects of Full Employment." *Political Quarterly* 14, no. 4 (1943): 322–31.

Kantorowicz, Ernst. *The King's Two Bodies: A Study in Medieval Political Theology*. Princeton, NJ: Princeton University Press, 2016.

Kotsko, Adam. *The Prince of This World*. Stanford: Stanford University Press, 2016.

———. "Repetition and Regression: The Problem of Christianity and Žižek's 'Middle Period.'" In *Repeating Žižek*, edited by Agon Hamza, 243–55. Durham, NC: Duke University Press, 2015.

———. "The Theology of Neoliberalism." In *Agamben's Coming Philosophy: Finding a New Use for Theology*, by Colby Dickinson and Adam Kotsko, 183–200. New York: Rowman and Littlefield International, 2015.

———. *Žižek and Theology*. New York: Clark, 2008.

Kramer, Heinrich, and James Sprenger. *Malleus Maleficarum*. Translated by Montague Summers. New York: Dover, 1971.

Krugman, Paul. "Infrastructure Build or Privatization Scam?" *The Conscience of a Liberal* (blog). *New York Times*, Nov. 19, 2016. https://krugman.blogs.nytimes.com/2016/11/19/infrastructure-build-or-privatization-scam/?mcubz=1.

Laclau, Ernesto, and Chantal Mouffe. *Hegemony and Socialist Strategy: Towards a Radical Democratic Politics*. 2nd ed. New York: Verso, 2014.

Lazzarato, Maurizio. *The Making of the Indebted Man: An Essay on the Neoliberal Condition*. Translated by Joshua David Jordan. Los Angeles: Semiotext(e), 2012.

Leshem, Dotan. *The Origins of Neoliberalism: Modeling the Economy from Jesus to Foucault*. New York: Columbia University Press, 2016.

Marley, Patrick. "Rep. Roger Rivard Criticized for 'Some Girls Rape Easy' Remark." *Milwaukee Journal-Sentinel*, Oct. 10, 2012. http://archive.jsonline.com/news/state-politics/state-legislator-criticized-for-comments-on-rape-hj76f4k-173587961.html.

McKenzie, Donald. "End-of-the-World Trade." *London Review of Books*, May 8, 2008, 24–26. www.lrb.co.uk/v30/n09/donald-mackenzie/end-of-the-world-trade.

Mills, Curt. "Sanders Says He'll Work with Trump on Trade: Credit Earned with Liberals like Sanders Is Met with Hesitation by Some in Trump's Own Party." *U.S. News and World Report*, Jan. 24, 2017. www.usnews.com/news/politics/articles/2017-01-24/bernie-sanders-says-hell-work-with-trump-on-trade-while-some-gopers-wary.

Mirowski, Philip. *Never Let a Serious Crisis Go to Waste: How Neoliberalism Survived the Financial Meltdown*. New York: Verso, 2013.

Monbiot, George. "Neoliberalism—The Ideology at the Root of All Our Problems." *Guardian*, April 15, 2016. www.theguardian.com/books/2016/apr/15/neoliberalism-ideology-problem-george-monbiot.

Mondzain, Marie-José. *Image, Icon, Economy: The Byzantine Origins of the Contemporary Imaginary*. Translated by Rico Franses. Stanford: Stanford University Press, 2005.

Moore, Lore. "Rep. Todd Akin: The Statement and the Reaction." *New York Times*, August 20, 2012. www.nytimes.com/2012/08/21/us/politics/rep-todd-akin-legitimate-rape-statement-and-reaction.html?mcubz=1.

Naas, Michael. *Derrida from Now On*. New York: Fordham University Press, 2008.

Nietzsche, Friedrich. *Genealogy of Morals*. Translated and edited by Walter Kaufmann. *Basic Writings of Nietzsche*. New York: Modern Library, 1992.

O'Neill, Kevin Lewis. *Cities of God: Christian Citizenship in Postwar Guatemala*. Berkeley: University of California Press, 2009.

Polanyi, Karl. *The Great Transformation: The Political and Economic Origins of Our Time*. Boston: Beacon, 2001.

Ramey, Joshua. *Politics of Divination: Neoliberal Endgame and the Religion of Contingency*. New York: Rowman and Littlefield International, 2016.

Rose, Marika. "After the Eschaton: *The Prince of This World* Book Event." *An und für sich*. April 27, 2017. https://itself.blog/2017/04/27/after-the-eschaton-the-prince-of-this-world-book-event/.

Rosza, Matthew. "Russia Attempted to Hack U.S. Voting Software Days Before Election: NSA Document." *Salon*, June 5, 2017. www.salon.com/2017/06/05/russia-attempted-to-hack-u-s-voting-software-days-before-election-nsa-document.

Santner, Eric. *The Royal Remains: The People's Two Bodies and the Endgames of Sovereignty*. Chicago: University of Chicago Press, 2011.

———. *The Weight of All Flesh: On the Subject-Matter of Political Economy*. Edited by Kevis Goodman. New York: Oxford University Press, 2016.

Schmitt, Carl. *The Concept of the Political*. Translated by George Schwab. Chicago: University of Chicago Press, 1996.

———. *The Nomos of the Earth in the International Law of the "Jus Publicum Europaeum."* Translated and edited by G. L. Ulmen. New York: Telos, 2003.

———. *Political Theology: Four Chapters on the Concept of Sovereignty*. Translated by George Schwab. Chicago: University of Chicago Press, 2005.

Taubes, Jacob. *The Political Theology of Paul*. Edited by Aleia Assmann and Jan Assmann. Translated by Dana Hollander. Stanford: Stanford University Press, 2004.

———. *To Carl Schmitt: Letters and Reflections*. Translated by Keith Tribe. New York: Columbia University Press, 2013.

Taylor, Mark C. *Confidence Games: Money and Markets in a World Without Redemption*. Chicago: University of Chicago Press, 2004.

Thayer, Richard H., and Cass R. Sunstein. *Nudge: Improving Decisions About Health, Wealth, and Happiness*. New Haven, CT: Yale University Press, 2008.

Tillich, Paul. *Dynamics of Faith*. New York: Harper Perennial, 2009.

Trott, Adriel M. "Nature, Action, and Politics: A Critique of Arendt's Reading of Aristotle." *Ancient Philosophy* 37, no. 1 (2017): 113–28.

Vogl, Joseph. *Specters of Capital*. Translated by Joachim Redner and Robert Savage. Stanford: Stanford University Press, 2014.

Zamora, Daniel, and Michael C. Bennett, eds. *Foucault and Neoliberalism*. New York: Polity, 2015.

Žižek, Slavoj. *The Sublime Object of Ideology*. New York: Verso, 1989.

INDEX